Sorrow Into Dancing!

Jey Samuel

ISBN 978-1-68570-005-8 (paperback)
ISBN 979-8-88616-723-8 (hardcover)
ISBN 978-1-68570-006-5 (digital)

Christian Faith Publishing
832 Park Avenue
Meadville, PA 16335
www.christianfaithpublishing.com

Printed in the United States of America

Contents

Comments of the Readers

I have posted my stories on Facebook for a few years. Below are the comments of those who have read my posts. Comments on Facebook are from my relatives, friends, and international students I have known over the years. These comments reflect their thoughts, feelings, and questions after reading my posts. Some posts were long, so I did cut them short and said, "See more." These comments are some, not all.

You also have the gift of writing & story-telling, so I still think you should write about all your dreams, in life & while you sleep!! So gifted Jey! You seem to me to be such a quiet, unassuming person, but you're a "dark horse"! 😊 (Colleen McLachlan)

Hi Jay, thank you for sharing your story. Beautifully written and enjoyed very much reading. Happy birthday. I hope things are well with you. (Susanta Singh)

I too enjoyed your story. Thanks for sharing it Jey! It's amazing how in these times we have the time to think back about others and events often a long time ago. I think we can something learn from these if we open our hearts. Guess that's a good thing. (Tim Hanst)

I am in awe with this story. Very beautifully said. Brings back memories. (Josh Cohen)

Great story! I read this part in your book. Really wonderful. (Christophe Lo)

Thank you for this beautiful story. I truly believe that God is my Refuge! I refuse to fear this virus or anything that comes my way. My God is a strong tower!

I also know without a doubt that it is He who numbers my days. (Joanie Fox)

Wow! This is a great story, our Lord is an amazing God! (Gemma Calicdan Dickerson)

Wow Jey! We've been friends with you and your family over 30 years and yet I'm learning so much about your Life through your writings...so beautifully written. I love the weaving of Scriptures in your reflections! I've always known you to be a kind, lo... (Linda Clark Elrod)

Awesome lovely to read your journey of life, mama (uncle). (Margaret Paul)

Thanks for sharing your story, Jey. I would really love to see some of your drawing. (Andrew Khoury)

Hi Jey! Thanks for your extremely descriptive experience of your exciting, fascinating and great activities your entire family enjoyed in Colorado!! I wish I could have been there!!! Thanks be to God for His Hand upon all of you in all your travels an… (Edward E. Samuel)

Beautiful story of God's faithfulness!! Very encouraging, Thank you Jey! (Rosemary Gillian)

Thanks for sharing such great insight to your life! (Reuben Kapadia)

I have always enjoyed reading your stories and this one is great! I still remember your stories about coming to the U.S. Thanks so much for sharing! (Elaine A. Scott)

Thank you for writing your special memories of His wonderful faithfulness. (Julie Chandler-Elrod)

Wonderful story and testimony, Mama. Keep doodling and painting! (Timothy Daniel)

I hope you will put all these together in a book. (Preeti Hannah Daniel)

Beautifully written mama(uncle). Enjoyed reading it and see how God has blessed you and used you in so many people's lives. (Kanchana Paul)

That is a great story Jey. (Roy Yabuki)

Great Jey! I really enjoyed this story. (Kurt Moore)

What a great story. (Joanie Fox)

Passion and zeal. (Jane Hays)

Good one! (Margaret Paul)

In His time... He makes all things beautiful in His time... (Sundari Paul)

This is beautiful Jey. Love Gods plan for our good! (Joanie Fox)

Jey I shared your story and I love ♡ your art. Stay safe. (Jane Hays)

Lovely story 😊 miss the old days. (Christophe Lo)

Nothing like camping except when there is a down pour and your tent is near a stream. But that rarely happens on earth. There are those who believe at the second coming Earth will be like heaven. Lovely dream Thanks for sharing it. (Mohan Sundareson)

So beautiful Jey! He does rejoice over us each day. (Joanie Fox)

Yes, Jay, you have loved international students well. Loved the story. (Sally Foster)

Very nice to hear about your student christian group. (Mohan Sundareson)

It is beautiful. (Andrew Khoury)

Great story Jey... PRAISE GOD. (Jim Boehm)

Wonderful story, mama. Thanks for sharing! (Philip Paul)

Yes, that is a great verse to go with this post!!! (Prakash Daniel)

"O Lord my God when I in awesome wonder" powerful testimony. Hard work is the secret of success! (Sundari Paul)

Jey, would you consider letting me share this story with my Sunday school class? We had a lesson on running the good race today and I think they'd like to read it. I would tell them you wrote it though! (Elaine A. Scott)

Lovely! Thank you. (Linda Clark Elrod)

A great lesson to everyone. Hard work and determination have great rewards! (Sundari Paul)

Awesome testimony mama 😍 Looking forward to more. (Margaret Paul)

Nice to have such wonderful friends, Jey. (Mohan Sundareson)

So beautiful Jey! He does rejoice over us each day. (Joanie Fox)

Very true mama🙏 (Margaret Paul)

Beautiful Jey. Needed thanks. (Jane Hays)

Enjoyed reading your posts…thought provoking. (Sundari Paul)

Wow, quite impressive and a wonderful analogy of the Christian race… Run the race, don't look back or around at others and trip or falter. Run with your eye on the goal! 🙏 (Linda Clark Elrod)

Angels. God's messenger from heaven. We can share the message of God's love and salvation. (Sundari Paul)

Please write a book... I agree with you, weddings in India is good seeing everyone in one place. (Sundari Paul)

Did Van Damm buy any of the houses? Jeyachandran your houses were always nicely designed and reasonably priced. (Mohan Sundareson)

Great story Jey!! Well done! (Elaine A. Scott)

Beautiful Jey! Thank you for sharing. I have actually lost things that I thought that I would never find again, and when I just happen upon them, I always look up and give thanks out-loud to God for finding them for me. OR better placing them in my path. (Kurt Moore)

Thanks Jey for that beautiful reminder. I wish most of my dreams were as beautiful! You should write a book about all the lovely dreams God gives you. Have a blessed Easter from our home to yours. God bless! (Colleen McLachlan)

Thanks so much. (Gemma Calicdan Dickerson)

Wow what an experience! I hope the other driver recovered? (Rosemary Gillian)

Miracle indeed. God protects His children. (Sundari Paul)

What a great story Jey! I am glad that Jesus protected you, but recounted it. (Elaine A. Scott)

🙏🙌Great testimony mama. (Margaret Paul)

He is ever faithful!!! An amazing story. (Cathy Makin)

Oh Jey, this is wonderful. I have missed reading your stories. Your description of places and emotions is excellent. Thank you so much for sharing! (Elaine A. Scott)

So nice to read about your trip. I had been in contact with a person in Nasik who wanted to buy my... (Mohan Sundareson)

Jesus paid it all. (SundarPaul)

Thanks Jey for sharing your story. Another confirmation that God never fails and is always there for us. (Dowie H. Crittenden Skip)

This was so awe-inspiring! I'm sure there are countless people who have encountered even more trials and difficulties, but you my Friend bless us all by acknowledging God's faithfulness through it all! What a comfort that He walks beside us and guides us ". This is the way, walk ye in it!" I would love to read of your conversion. Keep writing, I've created a saved file "Jey's stories". Blessings! (Linda Clark Elrod)

I always love your stories Jey. All of them are encouraging and because you use the word of God, it gives me lessons too. I can't wait for the next stories you will share. (Gemma Calicdan Dickerson)

Thank you, refreshing read. (Sundari Paul)

I remember this song! I used to sing it in a quartet decades ago! Thanks Jey! (Harry Brewer)

Adventure. (Jane Hays)

Jesus paid it all, all to Him I owe... Thank you, Jesus. (Sundari Paul)

Beautiful illustration Jey. (Kurt Moore)

Beautifully written. Could you share how you came to understand God's love for you? (Sally Foster)

During the last year in High School, I started attending Youth for Christ Rallies in Madras. One night at the end of Rally, one of the staff led me to accept Christ. That's how, I accepted His love personally. (Jey Samuel, in reply to the previous quote)

Wonderful testimony of God's providence and his constant guidance in our lives. (Timothy Daniel)

I am glad it was only a dream. Even if it was real God is always there to help. (Mohan Sundareson)

Absolutely beautiful! Thank you! (Linda Clark Elrod)

God provides. Miracles happen everyday. (Sundari Paul)

Good one! (Margaret Paul)

Me too. Or when I have lost/misplaced items, I simply say a prayer for the Lord to help me find them and that has not failed. 🙏 ♡ (Kurt Moore)

Wonderful! You're amazing! I've had bad nightmares from the time I was a child, so love it when I have the odd beautiful dream! I have had some lovely prophecy spoken over me, so the fact that your dreams are prophetic is just lovely. (Colleen McLachlan)

Love the story. (Gemma Calicdan Dickerson)

Journey with a powerful destination…reminds me of the song… "Chooku chooku, jeeva vandi." (Sundari Paul)

Introduction

Stories are magical. When I go back to when I was young and recollect my life, God's guidance has been incredible even when I was a kid. Years later, I realized that. Even though I wasn't aware of it, years later, year after year, the jigsaw puzzle of my life was woven together by the One who knows the beginning to the end. He knew me, and Psalm 139:16 (NKJV) tells me how in God's book, they all were written.

> *Your eyes saw my substance, being yet unformed.*
> *And in Your book they all were written,*
> *The days fashioned for me,*
> *When as yet there were none of them.* (Psalm 139:16 NKJV)

As I recollect each chapter in my life, I discover how each day was fashioned in such an intricate way by the One who made me. So years later, I recall, and as I write, God's spirit brings memories back. How much He loved me from the very start, how much He cared for me, even counting the hairs on my head as they grew and fell—they were all written in His book, and His spirit tells me from His written book to put them in this book. It is pure joy to recollect and thank Him for each day that He has given me. Even this recollection, as He brought many great memories, He may bring back memories even in your life—memories that you can even write and leave for your children and your children's children.

After I started to recollect and write stories, I realized how my memories began to come back. It is fascinating how I can remember the stories from years long ago. Now looking back, some of these instances were miracles that happened. Until I graduated high school, my medium of education was not English but Tamil. Then when I went to college, my major was architecture. So I never took English as one of my subjects, and it surprised me that I started writing in English. I was invited to a writer's group a few years ago, and I didn't know why I accepted the invitation. They started meeting at 9:00 p.m. on Friday evenings since some of them wanted to meet after the kids had gone to bed. And I also was volunteering with the international students group, which also met on Fridays at 7:00 p.m. Part of my volunteering included picking up and dropping them off. So depending on a Friday evening, which meant sometimes I would join them between 10:00 and 11:00 p.m.

When we met, each one of us needed to bring a chapter along with about ten copies. Most favored fiction. Each One would read what we brought, and everyone else would follow along with the copies. At times, someone stop the reading by asking questions or make comments. Everyone would also make comments or corrections on the copies they were given. Not being an English writer, I had many comments, modifications, and revisions from all the readers. That was my start. But I kept going back every Friday, most of the time, rewriting the same chapter I wrote before with the revisions. Just like what I did on my Bike Race, one of my chapters, persistence was my course of action, never giving up.

One Saturday, I had started reading my Bible for three hours; I enjoyed it very much. I decided to read it every morning for at least an hour. This made an exciting turn of events. God gave me some beautiful dreams, some things He showed me that were yet to happen, and some things that were beyond my wildest imaginations. All of them lined up with His Word, so I know He gave them. Not all

I received are in these chapters; I kept some of them for myself which I treasure.

God never forced me into anything, but when I reached out to Him, He came back with thunderous force loving me. After I started reading His Word at least for one hour each day, Jesus showed up early one morning, just before I opened my eyes. He was so bright in light that I was just awed with wonder till I heard my spirit shouting out, "I love You, Jesus!" That's when my spirit reached out to Him. A few days later, when I was reading my Bible and had my eyes closed, I saw the Father running toward me, hugged me, twirled me, and started kissing me. That showed how much He loved me. The more I reached out to Him, the more He reached out to me. The more I love Him, the more He loves me back. Even in busy days, I try to give the first hour of the day; I asked the Lord to fill me with His Holy Spirit and talk to me through His Word. By reading His Word, meditating on it, writing prayers, which I glance over during the day, my life has changed dramatically. Every moment of our life is orchestrated by God as we give ourselves to Him.

This is one of the books you don't have to start from the beginning and read through to the end. One day, you may decide you want to open it in the middle and read; go ahead. Each chapter is its own. You can start from the end and go backward. It is all in your hands how you want to read.

In the first part of my book, I did try to write stories from my younger days; then the latter part of my days. Then I share stories of what I shared previously and the other dreams He has given me. This book may never be finished. Even as I get more memories and dreams, I will be writing. As long as I keep loving Him, and He keeps loving me, there will be more to come. My Father is always working, so I will be writing as long as He keeps working in me. This is what Jesus had to say (in John 5:17 NIV), "Jesus said to them, 'My Father is always at his work to this very day, and I too am working.'"

As long as Jesus is working in my life, I will be writing… But it may come out in spurts, it may not come for a long time, I do not know, but He knows, and that's whom I trust.

We have become his poetry, a re-created
people that will fulfill the destiny he has
given each of us, for we are joined to Jesus,

the Anointed One. Even before we were
born, God planned in advance our destiny
and the good works we would do to fulfill it!
(Ephesians 2:10 TPT)

Look at the splendor of your skies,
your creative genius glowing in the heavens.
When I gaze at your moon and your stars,
mounted like jewels in their settings,
I know you are the fascinating artist who
fashioned it all!
But I have to ask this question:
Why would you bother with puny, mortal
man
or care about human beings?
Yet what honor you have given to men,
created only a little lower than Elohim,
crowned with glory and magnificence.
You have delegated to them
rulership over all you have made,
with everything under their authority,
placing earth itself under the feet of your
image-bearers.
All the created order and every living thing
of the earth, sky, and sea—

*the wildest beasts and all that move in the
paths of the sea—*
everything is in submission to Adam's sons.
Yahweh, our Sovereign God,
your glory streams from the heavens above,
*filling the earth with the majesty of your
name!*
People everywhere see your splendor! (Psalms
8:3–9 TPT)

This book has a lot of Bible quotations. For those who do not have a Bible, but want one, the Author is willing to send a Bible. For those who want to receive a Bible, please send an email with an address to SorrowIntoDancing@gmail.com.

For those who may have questions or comments, please send them to SorrowIntoDancing@gmail.com.

Acknowledgments

I am really thankful for the many that helped me in the process of writing this book. It will be impossible to name all who helped me in this process. Many have been instrumental in getting this book finished and made it possible for you to read.

First of all, I like to thank my family, who were involved in helping me in many tasks. I am also very grateful for the writer's group that I had been involved with; their input and creativity in many ways more than I can be grateful. I am deeply appreciative for the many others, who had given me advice at various times. I am indebted to all the leaders and students at International Students Inc. with whom I had been involved with over many years.

Above all, I thank my Lord, who gave me the words to write and all the resources to publish this book so I can share all that He has done for me.

I'm thanking You, God, from a full heart,
I'm writing the book on Your wonders.
I'm whistling, laughing, and jumping for
joy;
I'm singing Your song, High God. (Psalm
9:1 and 2 The Message)

1

The New Mindset: Sadness into Dancing!

What a dream, a dream come true. College days, days to remember, exciting times, then the excellent summer vacation toward the end. First-year in architectural school had been challenging but enjoyable. I loved my design and rendering classes. But solving problems in building structures and calculus wasn't my cup of tea.

In India, the exams at the end of the school year had the final say and were critical. So I studied hard, sometimes with no sleep at all. Toward the end, it was like a crescendo, the climax. My brain went through such high intensity that it was fried. But after the finals, there was that golden sunset, the vacation break.

At the end of my first year, ten friends decided to go to a camp at Nasik about one thousand miles from Madras (now Chennai, India). We also decided to spend a few more days in Bombay after Nasik. Wow! I looked forward to the day we left, a dream come true indeed. For an architectural student, Bombay was the height of architectural delight. Looking forward to this trip, my wait seemed like an eternity.

Finally, the day arrived. We left by train, staying on it overnight. Traveling in May, we found it to be the hottest month of the year and the most humid. We had seats in the lower class; all we could afford. Wooden bench seats, open windows, no air-conditioning, just hot, humid air, but still, having a wonderful time. There were ten best friends, and we had a great time together. Even when I slept sitting up on the wooden bench, it was still a thrilling experience. Just being with my friends, joking, and having fun conversations made it all the more enjoyable.

In those days, there were still some coal-burning locomotives that pulled the trains. They created lots of black smoke. All the windows in the compartment were open, so if you looked out of the window, you would get smoke in your eyes as well as little pieces of coal. The train wound through rice fields, over rivers, high bridges, forests, and mountains, and through tunnels. And even as the train went through a tunnel or the wind blew the smoke the wrong way, you got a whole load of these tiny pieces of ember in your eyes. Rub your eyes a little bit, and they became red. Regardless of the smoke or the glowing coal, I still liked to look out at the pretty countryside and the various scenes passing by.

My mind wandered. This is so great; I love it after all those finals and after all my hard work. I had an incredible feeling. Wow! Finals are over; it's so good to get away.

Every time the train would stop at a station, the vendors selling all kinds of food items shouted with a high-pitched voice whatever Indian delicacy they sold. One would be shouting "Puri, puri," another one, "Briyani, briyani," and another, "Chai, chai." So if you were hungry or thirsty, you would buy what you want to eat or drink and start eating once the train began to move again. One of my friends, Raj, was doing just that, eating.

Arasu asked Raj, "Hey, what did you buy?"

Sweating as he was, he replied, "I got this lamb briyani. It's so hot, and I'm perspiring so much!"

"But you are still eating…"

"It's awesome. Even though it's so spicy, the taste is so good. I never tasted anything so great."

Drops of sweat on his face looked like drops falling in monsoon rain. Giving him a bottle of water, Arasu said, "Raj, you better drink some water before you get ulcers."

"Thanks a lot. I just can't seem to stop eating. Ummm… ulcers? It's worth the risk."

His face got drenched even more after he started drinking the water. He looked as though he just came out of the shower. That is how we ate all through our journey, tasting all the food, some we never had before. Even during a hot summer day, we ate some of the hottest, spiciest food that was still foreign to us.

Yes, it was terrific. Augustine told me that the *puris* and *channa* were very good. Arasu was having some *kurma*. Having the same, I enjoyed every little bit of that as well.

The train journey fascinated me as we ventured into regions we had never seen before. Traveling with friends, we had a great time playing cards, enjoying it all. The sights, smell, and the sound of the locomotive were a new experience for me.

Even as the train would go through tunnels, it would sound a high-pitched whistle before it passed through. That sound would resonate in my eardrums for a while. And the scenery was incredible; from rice paddy fields to sometimes thick forest, one couldn't take one's eyes from the beautiful scenery. Yes, it was a great new adventure indeed.

On the way to Nasik, we had to change trains at Daund. Each of us had one suitcase, and there were about ten of us. When the train came to a screeching halt, the platform was buzzing with sounds. Vendors shouted the goods they sold, but we didn't know what they are saying. It was in a different language. Porters asked whether we wanted help with our luggage. We couldn't afford it, so we got off the train there and onto the platform, lined all the suitcases, and watched them. We had to wait for more than an hour for the connecting train.

Daund was a foreign city to me, so different. India, being very diverse, was fascinating to wait on the platform and watch all the men and women who dressed so differently. All the men wore different styles of clothes, mostly in white, and the women were in very colorful saris, worn quite differently. Other women wore *salwar kameez*, and children wore *pattu langa*. Some women sat in a row on the floor at the end of the platform, chewing something. The loudspeakers blasted music in a strange language. It was all so different and fascinating. I would have loved to have done a painting of this setting.

Madras to Daund was about seven hundred miles but looked like I was in a different country. Very little English was spoken in Daund; no one spoke Tamil, which we spoke. Marathi was spoken there, but none of us spoke it. Some knew Hindi and one or two of us spoke Hindi. So when we all got off at Daund, we had to talk to the very few that knew Hindi or English.

When the connecting train finally came, we saw it being fully packed. As before, we had the lowest class of seats. The doors were so crowded that we couldn't even enter through the doors. So we decided to board the train through the windows.

Some of my friends climbed up with the help of others and found places for our suitcases on the overhead racks.

The others watched our belongings on the platform and started passing our luggage one by one to us inside through the windows. We formed a human chain passing all our baggage into the train.

Suddenly the train conductor blew his whistle. We had to move fast to get our gear and all of us to get in. It started to move. The last one, Arasu, was still on the platform, went to get the last suitcase and shouted, "Can't find the last suitcase. Looks like somebody snatched it."

So Arasu, still on the platform, shouted again to all of us who were inside the train, "It's just not here. I'm going to stay and look for it. Keep going, get off at the next station, and wait for me. I'll meet you at the next station."

The train started pulled away. Arasu stayed back, looking for the missing suitcase. We all got off at the next station and waited for him. He came by the next train and told us, "I ran up and down the platform but couldn't find the suitcase. I just had to report it to the police. Can we all check whose it was?"

"Got my gear," "Found my trunk," most of them shouted.

But I couldn't find mine. It was mine that was stolen. My heart sank; my jaw dropped. Everything I owned was in that suitcase—all my clothes, my nightwear, even money for expenses, my toiletries and everything for my three-week trip; on me was just a few rupees left in my pocket and my train ticket.

I had a panic attack and was in despair, like slamming on the brakes (when going full speed) coming to a screeching halt; my heart had a heavy pounding and then stopped.

All sorts of negative thoughts circled my mind. One set of clothes? How am I going to survive the next three weeks? Not much money left. What am I going to do? What if my parents found out?

So many questions flooded my mind. Even with all my friends around me, I felt alone. My mouth had utterly dried up. Speechless, I stood, with a blank stare on my face.

So we found out what was the next station bound for Nasik and left on that train. That train, too, was crowded, but we all managed to get on the train.

I felt isolated and devastated in the crowded train, with all the people around me and only standing room left. Negative thoughts overwhelmed me. How am I going to manage? Lost everything. Even as fire can cause water to boil, my negative thoughts fueled my mind to a boiling point.

These thoughts just kept coming back into my mind. My enjoyment of the train ride suddenly disappeared, and when I looked out of the window, everything was just a blur. I still had about two weeks at Nasik, another week in Bombay, and my return trip.

Everyone felt bad for me. All promised to pitch in. But we were all students, and everyone was on a very tight budget. Even among friends, I felt so lonely, sad, abandoned, and forsaken.

My mind couldn't get away from these thoughts, which kept nagging me. I can't remember much except my stolen suitcase and the rest of my memory being washed out. All the sights, sounds, and the excitement of travel suddenly evaporated. I was so lost in my thoughts. Memory eclipsed by; loneliness haunted me. All my pleasant memories were thrown out. A feeling of helplessness filled my mind.

I became so lonely; I felt discouraged and depressed. It seemed like I lost everything I had. But at that time, suddenly a Bible verse stood out, in my mind, "For Jesus had said, "I will never leave you, nor forsake you" (Hebrews 13:5p NKJV); I had already accepted Christ and was a child of His. But I was still growing in my relationship with Him. So it was just momentary loneliness I was facing and showed my immaturity. Did I forget, "He is with me, here, next to me?"

In my loneliness on the wooden bench seat in the train, when I realized that I still had Christ, that is when my spiritual eyes opened up.

Another verse in the Bible came to me, "Whatever I have, wherever I am, I can make it through anything in Jesus who makes me who I am" (Philippians 4:13 The Message). Yes, I can make it through anything. Why should it matter that much when I lose my luggage?

Jesus is all that I need. His love for me would never change. My thoughts of dependence on Him changed my mindset. My negative thoughts and feelings of loneliness melted away. Another verse showed up: "For when I am weak, then I am strong" (2 Corinthians 12:10 NKJ). I realized that Christ would fill all my voids, even in my worst circumstances, and make me strong to withstand my negative thoughts. When I knew that in Him there is the protection of God's heavenly army all around me, my mind relaxed.

Once my mindset changed from loneliness to one relying on Christ, my whole trip became different. So when I went to the camp in Nasik, I had a wonderful time there and in Bombay. I enjoyed the entire journey. It didn't matter that I had only one set of clothes, and I didn't have any extra money to spend. I never wondered what others thought of me wearing the same clothes day after day. I was no longer the victim but became a victor.

Soon after my luggage was lost, someone else gave me a Bible to replace the one that I'd lost. That was all that I needed. Many were the promises in the Bible that I went time and time again to read them. I never found my luggage, but that didn't matter. There was another whole world for me to grasp. I had Jesus; that was all that mattered. He changed my sorrow into dancing.

You changed my sorrow into dancing.
You took away my clothes of sadness,

and clothed me in happiness.
I will sing to you and not be silent.
Lord, my God, I will praise you forever.
(Psalm 30:11–12 New Century Version)

As I got used to living with one set of clothes and enjoyed what I had, nothing mattered to me but knowing Jesus was with me all the time, which made a world of difference to me. I had written home about what had happened, so when I arrived, they were fine with it and glad I was back with them. And I had all the stories of my trip to tell them like how God was with me and made me dance with "a song as that in the day of a feast"!

LORD JEHOVAH your God within you, the Mighty Man and The Savior, He shall sweeten you in joy and He shall make you new in his love, and He shall make you dance with a song as that in the day of a feast! (Zephaniah 3:17 PHBT)

2

How I Like What I Do

Growing up in India as a kid, birthdays were quite different. There weren't many presents, nor any parties, and no big cakes with candles to blow out. It was a small get-together with just close family singing the birthday song, exchanging simple gifts, hugs, and kisses.

Being the youngest one in the family, having four older sisters, and being the only son, I received lavish gifts from them all every birthday. Even as my dad traveled to big cities and came back, he would bring me something exotic. I looked forward to every birthday, and I loved it.

When the time came to celebrate one of my sister's birthdays, I didn't have any money as a little kid. I wasn't able to give them any presents. That made me a little sad;

I felt awkward. I thought I wasn't able to do anything for them in return.

So for their birthdays, I first started writing silly stories. They laughed since they were so foolish. Then I started doing doodles and gave them my strange drawings. Whatever I gave my sisters, they appreciated. They thanked me and hugged me. As years went by, my pictures started to get better and better.

My father went to Madras, the capital of my state, and bought me a watercolor set on one of my birthdays. I taught myself to paint. As every birthday approached, I would paint and give my sisters different paintings. I also started to do it for fun, getting better and better. It became one of my hobbies.

My dad bought me a Mechano set, like Legos, and I got involved with it on my sixth birthday. I built little toys like houses and cranes, etc. You would attach various plates with screws and bolts like an erector set.

Before starting high school, we moved to Madras. My brother-in-law was a civil engineer who lived in Neyveli, about one hundred miles from us. He was always into innovations, and I found him very interesting. His brother was posted in Washington with the World Bank and invited my brother-in-law to go there and do his postgraduate education.

He had gone to study for his master's in architecture in the United States. After he came back from the US, he visited our home on the weekend. He came to my room, and I was working on my Mechano set.

When he saw me, we had a great conversation. I was in my pre-university year then.

"Thumby [younger brother], how are you doing?" he asked. "I have seen some of your paintings you gave Dulcie [my sister]. They are outstanding. I think you should do architecture."

"What are you talking about? What is architecture?"

"That's what I went to study in the States. You know, designing buildings and houses."

"Sounds interesting."

"I'll leave some books and magazines about architecture with you so you can look at them."

"Thanks!" I said, with my attention now piqued.

I liked what I saw in those books. I started enjoying American architecture; I had never seen anything like it in India. I talked to my dad about it. But my father was set on me being an engineer.

A few months went by. I was applying to the engineering college. I also found that the University of Madras had just started a School of Architecture. So I asked my father whether I could apply there as well. My father was very hesitant and turned down my request.

I never gave up but kept up a positive spirit in all my conversations with my dad. Then I had my brother-in-law speak to him. After quite a while, my dad agreed. So I applied for both engineering and architecture.

For admission to the Engineering College, I sent all that they had asked for. Still, with the advice of my brother-in-law and my grades, I sent a portfolio of my watercolor paintings and black and white drawings for architecture.

I had to wait for quite a while. Finally, I got an invitation from both schools for an oral interview. I went to both. Each had a panel of four or five professionals. Both panels asked me why I would want to become an engineer or an architect.

At the Engineering College interview, I told them of my interest in Mechano sets and building various models. I gave a similar answer at my interview at the Architecture School, adding my interest in drawings and painting. I explained how I got interested in my brother-in-law's conversation in law and my interest in art and architecture, and how he became an architect. A panelist pulled one of my paintings that I had submitted, stared at it, and then he passed it on to the others. They seem to like what they saw.

I had to wait for a while to get my results. I got a letter from the engineering college I had admission there, and my dad was pleased. But I still wanted to find out from the architecture school. Finally, I received this letter, and I got accepted there as well. I was delighted and showed it to my dad. But he wasn't thrilled.

My father told me the reason for his hesitancy, and it was because he didn't think there would be many prospects for architects in India. He felt engineers had much more excellent opportunities. I kept a positive attitude with him but reached out again to my brother-in-law to talk to my dad.

Then my father found out he knew one of the panelists for the Architecture School. He set an appointment and went to see him. After he came back from seeing him, he said I could join the School of Architecture at the University of Madras. That took me totally by surprise!

I asked my dad what changed his mind. He told me that the panelist said there were about six thousand applicants for Architecture School, but there was room for only twenty students, and I was one of the twenty selected. My dad had asked the panelist whether there was anything special with the selection process. He said many applicants had higher scores in math and science, but I was one of the few that had submitted color paintings and drawings, and they were impressed. The panelist told my dad, architects must know how to sketch and draw as well. After they had seen my art, they voted me in.

I was taken back. I was one of those that got selected out of the six thousand applicants? God's hand was on me on this one.

The panelist also assured my dad he didn't have to worry about the prospects for architects in India. As more graduated, the need for engineers who have been doing the drawings for buildings would diminish as more architects would be taking their place. So my dad told me I could join Architecture School. I was so happy.

How I love what I do. My client gives me what I need, and I imagine the solution. I keep doing doodles and sketches of what I imagine could be the solution. I would make a model to finalize what I had imagined, my imagination would get built, and I would enjoy the outcome. Once completed, there was an internal satisfaction on how the final product looked in three dimensions compared to what I had imagined and designed.

> *"11I know the plans I have for you,"*
> *says the Lord. "I want you to enjoy success.*
> *I do not plan to harm you. I will give you*
> *hope for the years to come. 12Then you will*
> *call out to me. You will come and pray to*
> *me. And I will listen to you. 13When you*
> *look for me with all your heart, you will find*
> *me." (Jeremiah 29:11–13 NIRV)*

Over the years, I knew it was the Lord that had plans for me. He did want me to enjoy success as He promised. He gave me hope for years to come, as in the promise. He created me for His good pleasure, and I enjoy what He enjoys. I rejoice in what He did with my life, as He rejoices over me.

> *Every single moment You are thinking of me!*
> *How precious and wonderful to consider*
> *that You cherish me constantly in Your every*
> *thought!*
> *O God, Your desires toward me are more*
> *than the grains of sand on every shore!*
> *When I awake each morning, You're still*
> *with me.* (Psalm 139:17–18 Passion Tr.)

It is incredible to think that God of earth and heaven is always thinking of me and designing me, even before I was born, creating me with numerous cells, parts, and directing my path for my good. So when I get in tune with Him, He even works for my better good. He plans for my success.

Knowing He is constantly thinking of me, my future is bright, with many thoughts and designs for my good. It is way beyond what you would do for your child, how you would want them to become a success. But God in His infinite wisdom can do for me, far beyond what I can think, dare even to ask, or even dream in my wildest imagination!

"Now glory be to God, who by his mighty power at work within us is able to do far more than we would ever dare to ask or even dream of—infinitely beyond our highest prayers, desires, thoughts, or hopes" (Ephesians 3:20 TLB).

3

Miracle in London

Five years had gone by faster than a bullet train. There were many great days, some intensive days in studies and some grueling days in exam halls. They went so fast. And college days were over. Crazy days of joking around with friends, leaving all those memories of good times were a thing of the past. All my friends were going in different directions. Studying also was a thing of the past.

Now it was time to find a job. And I received a great offer from a top British architectural firm called Prynne, Abbott, and Davis. It was incredible. It was from one of the well-known firms in Madras. The offer for me was to be a project designer.

An Englishman and an Indian owned the firm. Between the two, they were able to get some great projects for the firm. As the Indian partner would meet with a client, he would sketch the plans upside down for the clients to see sitting across the table. They were very fascinated by his talent. The head of the design group was a great designer. It was an incredible experience for me, right out of college designing the projects that I used to only dream of.

A year went by. One day, my dad called me by my nickname, "Thumby [younger brother], how are you? Are things going fine at work?"

"Yes, Dad, work is great. I like what I am doing."

"So does that mean you are stable in your job and ready to settle down?"

"Not quite yet, Dad. I've been thinking of doing graduate studies."

He asked me with some hesitation, "Does the University of Madras have a master's program in architecture?"

"No, Dad, only master's in planning, but I want to do architecture."

"So where do they have the graduate program you want to do?"

"You know I checked all the universities in India, and they are only planning to start one in the future, none right now."

He hesitated. "So, Thumby, that means you have to travel abroad?"

"Yes, Dad. I want to go to the US. I love American architects and their design. I would love to study there."

His tone got softer. "You know, Thumby, we can't afford to send you abroad. It is so expensive for fees and living."

I stammered even as I spoke. "Yes, I know. I also found out that the exchange allowed now out of India is only fifty rupees, that's only ten dollars. That's just enough for a taxi ride. So not only do I need admission, but I also have to get a scholarship or assistantship to study there."

He was curious. "What is an assistantship?"

"Well, when you do graduate work, the university also can hire you to assist the professor help with the under-graduate students. That way, they would also help me with tuition and living expenses."

His answer was just silence.

Being last in a family of five, I was the only boy and the last one left at home. After having four daughters ahead of me, my mom and dad had wanted a son. So now you can understand why the silence.

It was hard for my parents and sisters to think of me leaving home and flying to the other side of the globe, about ten thousand miles away. All my sisters had gotten married; guess who the only one left was.

It took a while. Then my parents talked to me some more after a few days. Then finally, my dad gave me the nod.

My research started in applying for graduate studies. I made several trips to the US Consulate in Madras. My thoughts: *An uncertain future perhaps, unknown venture, many uncertain conditions. Where do the funds come from?*

Who can I turn to? A lonely journey, could go broke, could go haywire. Do I want to do this? My thoughts were all over the place.

I was reading my Bible, and a verse spoke to me, as in Psalm 37:5, "Commit your way to the Lord; trust and be confident also in Him and He will act on your behalf."

I found out that there were master's programs at the University of Kansas and the University of Oklahoma which also offered assistantships. These available programs could pay for my tuition and living expenses, so I applied to both schools. I received acceptance letters from both universities, but only University of Oklahoma offered me an assistantship. My only cost was my plane ticket; I could just sell my scooter to pay for the flight.

Was I ever excited and happy! The great news that I've been waiting for! I was on the mountaintop. After talking with my parents, I replied to the University of Oklahoma. I accepted both the admission and the assistantship, so I began the preparations for the trip.

However, after a month, there was another letter from the university. Due to the shortage of funds, they had to cancel my assistantship but wrote that I could still attend the university by paying the fees. My hopes were dashed, my dreams in the dumpster.

Being so disappointed, I had to cancel all my plans to go to the US. From a crescendo of excitement, this was a significant letdown for me. Like David in the Bible, I had cried, my cry was the same, "Be not far from me, O Lord; You are my help, hasten to help me." Yet I read another verse in James 1:2, "Consider it pure joy whenever you face various trials." However, instead of brooding over my disappointment, I began to share my disappointment with a few people I knew closely.

Among other people, I met one of my friends. He was from Canada. He was a leader of a youth group.

"Hey, Bob, how are you?"

"Thanks for asking. How are your plans to study in the States?"

I shared my disappointment. "Bob, I got a letter from the University of Oklahoma. They had their funds cut, and so they canceled my assistantship. They told me that my admission is good, but I've to pay the fees. You know I don't have funds."

"Have you ever thought about working and going to graduate school at the same time, as Canadian and American students usually do?"

I was inquisitive. "How would that be possible for me?"

He answered my question with a question. "Didn't you tell me you have an architectural degree and you've worked for a British firm for two years?"

"Yes, that's true."

"My sponsor, Ray Stevens, lives in Calgary, and I'll give him a call and talk to him about finding a job for you there. I think it is easy for architects to find a job in Canada. There is the University of Alberta in Calgary, where you could study and work simultaneously. How about giving me your resume tomorrow?"

"Yes, I'll bring it to you tomorrow. Wow, thanks so much, Bob."

So I saw him the very next day with my resume. And he sent it to Ray Stevens in Calgary. When Stevens received it, he looked up all the architect's names in the Yellow Pages and saw fifty of them. So he made fifty copies of my resume and mailed one to each of them.

Surprise! Surprise! One of the biggest firms in Calgary wrote to me in India, telling me that they were offering me an architectural designer's job and would help in whatever way they could for me to obtain a visa to go to Canada. Was that an answer to my prayer? I remembered a verse in the Bible: "God works in mysterious ways His wonders to perform" (Habakkuk 1:5 KJV) Being excited again, I gave the good news to Bob, and he congratulated me.

Finding out that getting a visa to Canada meant going to New Delhi, the capital of India, about one thousand miles away. Obtaining a visa could take up to a year brought discouragement again. Would the architectural firm in Calgary that made the offer wait for a year? Facing a mountain again, my prayer to God was for direction and help. "Lord, You did a miracle getting me into Architectural School. So my next step is Yours." My faith began to build. My conversation with a few of my friends focused on my next step.

Then I met another friend of mine. "Hey, Prabaker, what are you up to these days?"

His immediate question was, "How are your plans to go to the US for graduate work?"

"They canceled my assistantship. But now, I do have an offer from an architectural firm in Canada. I'm told it'll take a year to get a work permit. I'm not sure whether the firm will wait for me for that long."

"Maybe not. I've another suggestion for you. I just found this out. If you have a professional degree and two years of work experience, you could obtain a work permit and visa to England in two weeks. You've got an architectural degree and worked over two years with a British firm. That's all you need. You know, once in England, it would take only two to three months to get a visa to Canada from there because they've got a special relationship."

"Thanks for the news. Sounds very interesting. I'll go to the British Consulate and see if I can get a visa. I'll also have to see if they have any postings for jobs in England. Thanks again."

So I went there, and they told me the same. It sounded great. And I looked for any postings for architects in England but didn't see any. Knowing there were no jobs for me in England, I wondered, *How was my comfort level in having landed in London with fifty rupees and no work, and with only the promise of work in Canada? Was I ready to take the plunge?*

Taking a bold step of faith, I decided to go anyway to England. I received support from everybody around me, including my parents. But God was in the planning all along. By faith, my steps were planted. Paraphrasing Hebrews 11:1 (CEV), "Faith makes me sure of what I hope for and gives me proof of what I cannot see."

I wrote to the Canadian firm about my plans, and they were okay with it. They assured me that they would help me in any way to obtain my Canadian visa.

Finally, the great day arrived. Taking off from the Madras Airport with an equivalent of ten dollars, I arrived in Rome for a day of stay. My friend had an uncle, Mr. Raj, who was pretty high up in the Indian Embassy in Rome, and he had arranged for me to stay with his uncle for the day. So when I arrived in Rome, a chauffeur was waiting at the airport with my name on a board for me to see. He took me to a mansion in Rome, where I received the royal treatment at Mr. Raj's home.

After a sumptuous breakfast at his home, Mr. Raj also had arranged for his chauffeur to take me to see all the incredible sights of Rome. The chauffeur took me to lunch at a sidewalk café near the Vatican. Mr. Raj also gave me a royal dinner that night. My level of excitement had reached a very high point. I had thoroughly enjoyed that day. Early next morning, the chauffeur took me back to the airport.

Then as I was checking in at the airport, the flight attendant asked me, "Mr. Samuel, I see you're going to London. Please place your two suitcases on the weighing scale.

So I did.

Then she said, "Mr. Samuel, you have excessive baggage. I'll let you know what you have to pay."

My heart sank. "What's next, Lord?"

"Madam, I had this checked in Bombay for an international flight. They told me then that the weight was within limits. I haven't added anything in Rome."

"No discussions, Mr. Samuel. We go by our weighing scale. You have excess baggage, and your payment is 1,100 Lire. You can pay that at the cashier there and bring me the receipt if you want to leave."

So I gave them half of what I had. From a high point of seeing Rome, now I had my lows of what my future held. My prayer was, *Lord, still, You've got the best waiting for me.*

Eventually landing in London, I took the bus (there goes half a Pound) to the Indian YMCA, where my dad had arranged for me to stay for free until my first paycheck. Only breakfast and dinner were served there. So I was always the last to have breakfast and the first one to show up for dinner, never having had lunch. Changing the one pound that was left into shillings and pennies to make the phone calls on the payphone to find a job, I walked all over London for interviews, trying to save the pennies that were left.

I looked every morning for a job posting at the YMCA and called all day long as I thought there might be an opening for me. Every time I made a phone call to apply for a job, one on the other end could be a Welsh, a Scot, an Irish, or a person with a strong Cockney accent. Trying to understand all the accents were intricate, and they also had problems with my Indian accent. Then after getting an appointment, finding the address was the other challenge. There could have been 30 Windsor streets, one in SW 1, NE 4, etc., but if I made one error in understanding, I would end up ten miles from the location where the interview would have been, having walked in the wrong direction.

Those were lonely days. I was homesick—nobody to talk to, no one to listen to, no advice to give or be given, no calls from home or friends since I didn't have a phone. I would even cry at times. But during those lonely days, there was God's presence; the cries of David in Psalms were a comfort to me. God was there for me no matter what, no matter where, always within reach of a whisper. But I knew that God brought me to London, and I was very thankful to Him.

I went to Him to lean on even in my loneliness. He gave me His shoulders to lean on and heard my cry; in desperation, I did not understand the Cockney or the various accents, getting lost without anyone giving me directions.

Reading my Bible was a natural source of comfort during those lonely days. The many promises in the Bible shone like the many stars in the sky for me; the many trees in the forest. They were numerous to count. I just banked on them. It gave me the strength to face the loneliness and uncertainty of the next day.

On the fourth day, I had an appointment for an interview with Mr. Jones at 4:00 p.m. in Ealing, about eight miles from the YMCA. I started walking at around 1:00 p.m. to the interview. It started raining, and since my material for the interview included a big roll of blueprints, I decided to take a risk with my little bit of money and take the subway part of the way. It didn't take long before getting on the other end, but it was a downpour, raining pretty heavy when I got out of the subway. I waited at the station under the shelter for a while so the rain would slow down. But being in a hurry, with the clock ticking, I couldn't wait any longer.

Getting out of the station, I ran out, getting thoroughly soaked. Without a map and not being able to see the signs in the dark, I was lost. In the pouring rain, I could not ask anyone for direction. The rain lightened down, and finally, I found the correct address at 4:55 p.m., but my appointment was for 4:00 p.m. Just as I reached the entry hall, I overheard a conversation.

"It's almost five o'clock. Mr. Samuel hasn't shown up. I'm going to leave now. If he calls or shows up, reschedule the appointment for tomorrow. If he can't come tomorrow, tell him that the post has gotten filled. I'm a little upset. It's almost an hour late, and he hasn't even got the decency to call me."

"Okay, Mr. Jones, I'll let him know what you told me."

So I walked in and approached both of them.

"Mr. Jones, I'm terribly sorry that I'm so late. It has been such pouring rain that I couldn't see any street signs in the dark, and I totally got lost. I've been in London only four days, and even though I started around 1:00 p.m., from Brighton, I could finally find it only now. I'm so sorry."

He stared at me up and down. "Mr. Samuel, you're soaking wet. It must be raining cats and dogs outside. I can see the reason why you're so late. Now that you're here, why not come inside and take off that drenched coat."

"Thank you so much, Mr. Jones. It's so kind of you to see me, being so late."

"Well, can you hand me your resume?"

So I gave him my resume. He took his time reviewing it.

"So you worked for a British firm after you graduated. Can you give me more details of some of the projects you've worked, and to what extent you were involved in design?"

So I told him all of the projects I had worked on and my involvement at the firm I worked.

"What made you leave the firm and leave for Britain?"

"I wanted to do graduate work before too long. There aren't any programs in India, so I thought I would go abroad, work, save funds, and then do my master's."

"That seems to be a good reason... Now let me see your drawings." His British manners were apparent when I handed him my drawings. "Oh no! My! Good heavens! The drawings are soaked as well. Let me see them anyway."

So I opened the drawings, and he reviewed the few drawings that were not too wet. He seemed surprised. "They seem fairly good. Too bad some of them are so wet. I would've liked to see them all. So have you started saving for your studies yet?"

"Pretty badly. When I left India, they would allow me to take out only fifty rupees, about three pounds. After paying excess baggage fees and bus fares, I landed at the YMCA with only a pound. Now I've been using that to make the phone calls and subway fare. I have been walking everywhere. The funds that I had have been disappearing very quickly."

"Quite a story! You know, Mr. Samuel, we have two positions open here, just like we have advertised. I've already seen over thirty applicants. Most of them have a much better experience than you. But I think you need the job more than anyone else. From what I have seen and heard, you'll do just fine here. So be here at 9:00 a.m. tomorrow and be ready to start working. It pays thirty pounds a week starting tomorrow for you."

Wow! I was taken aback by his surprise offer. "Thank you so much, Mr. Jones. I appreciate the time you took to see me even though I delayed you so much, so you've had to stay so late. Thanks so much, again."

I felt like hugging him but, being civil, just shook his hands and left. Then outside in the rain, I was dancing with joy. Wow! What a surprise! From sorrow into dancing! That indeed was a miracle.

All I can say is that even with getting lost, being confused, and being so anxious about getting there so late, God was with me all the time, and He always came through for me. He worked out things for me without me even being aware of them. Every time an event like this happened, it confirmed my faith in Jesus more and more. One day I was getting to my last pennies, and the next day, I get a job that starts paying.

I was in London for seven weeks and had the same job until I left after getting my visa to Canada. Having saved up enough money for the trip, I was on the plane to Calgary. Being in London all those weeks, though I was lonely, I had my Bible and my Jesus all along, also knowing that Jesus was by my side all the time. I was His child. This also helped me enjoy my stay in London. That was a fascinating experience for me to be in London. The sights and sounds did overwhelm me at times.

Amazement was the word. Astonishment, marvelous, awe, stunned, and dumbfounded could have been more words to explain how things worked out even though there were disappointments at times. There were so many ups and downs, so many valleys I looked down as well as many mountains I faced. But God was with me all the time. I was dumbfounded by how it all turned out.

I came across verses in the Bible (Isaiah 40:4–8): "Every valley shall be exalted, and every mountain and hill brought low...all flesh is grass...the grass withers, the flower fades, but the word of our God stands forever."

Over and over, my faith grew stronger, and my trust in God solidified. I knew God's Word stands forever. Every circumstance was different. I did face various challenging circumstances, but when I trusted God and read His word, He gave me the strength to overcome every problem. I did have a fear of the unknown, but I took every circumstance to God and left it with Him. "Leave all your worries with him, because He cares for you" (1 Peter 5:7 GNT).

God knows every turn that's ahead of me, every road-block I would face, but when I placed my trust in Him, He took care of my every need. God is a God of completion;

when you cry out to Him and ask for all your needs and direction, He completes what He started in your life and is an awesome God. He knows the end of your journey from the beginning. You can fully trust Him to come through for you when you ask Him. You'll never regret the step you took to trust Him.

The Psalmist in the Bible said, "He who lives in the secret place of the Most High will rest in the shadow of the Almighty. I will say of the Lord, "He alone is my refuge and my place of safety, my God, in whom I trust" (Psalm 91:1–2).

When you can see the invisible God and live in the secret place of His presence, miracles can happen; you can't see the wind, but when the wind blows, you can only see the rustling of the leaves. When it blows, it can also uproot the trees. You don't want loneliness and hurt to overcome you, but instead, you want to overcome loneliness and hurt when God is on your side.

I found for myself repeatedly that whatever I faced, when I trusted Him, He came through for me. He was working behind the scene all the time and worked out everything for me. The more I had my needs met, the more

I trusted God, the more I trusted Him; my faith in God grew more assertive. He is my Daddy; I am His child.

You can be lonely; you could be crying right now, wondering what to do next. Many circumstances can be challenging; this virus is unknown; every problem may be different. But in every case, when I had trusted Jesus to come through, He did. I saw myself as His child. I saw myself through His eyes as a Father looking at His child. Will you let your child down? Will, He let you down as His child? He is an awesome God. He will never let you down.

All I can say is "wow" when you take and leave all things to God and trust in His promises for you in the Bible. It's an incredible feeling. The promises are like stars in a dark, clear night twinkling even as you stare at them. Have you ever gazed at the stars at night and had an incredible feeling of being lost in them? Trusting God and being lost in Him gave me the same awesome feeling. He gave me the joy down in my heart.

"Though you have not seen Him, you love Him; and though you do not even see Him now, you believe and trust in Him and you greatly rejoice and delight with inexpressible and glorious joy" (1 Peter 1:8 AMP).

4

Guess Who Took the Blame

"Thumby, want to drive?" (Thumby was my nickname.)

"What? Are you crazy?" I asked.

This happened when I went to high school in India. One day, when my driver came to pick me up from school, he called me by my nickname and opened the driver's door.

"Don't you want to learn to drive today? I can teach you," he asked me.

"Drive this car? But I'm only fourteen!"

My voice was hesitant.

"It's not that hard. Get in. I'll show you," he replied.

I was all excited but at the same time scared to death.

I got in and looked at all the pedals, the accelerator, the brake pedal, and the clutch. It was scary. I thought, *There are too many!*

So I told him, "I can't handle all of these pedals!" And never even thought about what my father would say if I were to drive.

"I will take care of all of those." He said, "All you have to do is to handle the steering wheel. Just look straight at the road and turn the steering wheel when you see the curve in the road. That's all you have to do."

He made it so easy. I adjusted myself in the seat.

"Can you see the road?" he asked.

"Yes, I can."

"Put your hands on the steering wheel. All you have to do is turn that wheel." He was confident I could drive— made it easy, like riding the bike.

"I can do that."

"Now I'm going to sit on the passenger's seat. I'll handle the accelerator, the brake, the clutch, and the stick shift. You handle the steering," he said.

Both his feet stretched over to the accelerator and the brake.

"I'm ready. Just let me know when I'm doing wrong," I said, pumped with excitement.

"We'll practice first in this empty parking lot, so you can learn how to steer before we hit the road," he said.

"Good idea," I said.

We drove on the parking lot, and I seem to do fine. Then we slowly proceeded to the road.

The road was narrow, but still, the going was good.

As we were driving along, about halfway to our house, suddenly, I saw my dad walking toward us on the other side of the road. (I forgot that was the route for his daily walk.)

I froze. I panicked. I ducked my head below the dashboard. I didn't want my dad to see me driving at all costs.

"What are you doing?" the driver shouted. "You can't duck your head when you are driving."

"My dad is walking toward us on the other side. I don't want him to see me behind the wheel. That's why I ducked," I stammered.

"Okay, calm down, I'll take care of the wheel," he said as he leaned over from the passenger's seat and took the steering wheel as well.

I was still full of fear hoping my dad wouldn't find out.

After we passed my dad, the driver said, "We have gone past your dad. Let's pull to the side."

We pulled over and stopped. We switched seats, and he drove me home.

About half an hour later, my dad came home from his walk. He went straight to the driver and started screaming at him.

He was at the top of his voice. "Why were you driving the car with your whole body and head tilted? Were you drunk? You would've been in big trouble if you had crashed my car."

The driver remained silent. He never told my dad it was me at the steering wheel.

My dad never found out who was the guilty one. I was the one. I felt so bad. I should have told my dad that I was at fault, but I never did. I lied to my dad by omission and did nothing for the innocent man. But the driver took the blame for me.

I was at fault. What I had done was wrong, but the driver could have easily avoided being scolded and could have pointed at me. And I could have taken the brunt of my dad's anger. And it could have been brutal.

In the same way, for all the things I have done in my life, the bad stuff, the wrong things, my sins, I have done, had God-given me the punishment I deserved, how severe, how brutal it could be. God's wrath could be devastating to me. But this is what the Bible tells me.

"Jesus is the one who took God's wrath and blame against our sins upon Himself and brought us into fellowship with God; and He is the forgiveness for our sins, and not only ours but all the world's" (1 John 2:2).

That's incredible. Jesus took my blame; He took my punishment. He was the sacrifice for me. The Gospel is the good news for me; once I accepted that Jesus took my sins on the cross, I am forgiven. Just like the driver took all the yelling from my dad, his anger went on the driver. All I could do was watch his anger go on the driver. It was the same way; God's anger and wrath went on Jesus, as long as I accepted Him taking my place.

So now, for all the wrongs I have done, I have accepted what Jesus did for me on the cross, and I believe I'm forgiven, I'm acquitted, and I thank Him for taking my punishment on Himself for me. Everlasting life means, even after I die, I live with Him in heaven and enjoy all the joys of heaven as well—what an incredible life!

This is how much God loved the world:
He gave his Son, Jesus, His one and only
Son. And this is why: so that no one need be

destroyed; by believing in him, anyone can have everlasting life.

God didn't go to all the trouble of sending his Son merely to point an accusing finger, telling the world how bad it was. He came to help, to put the world right again.

Anyone who trusts in him is acquitted; anyone who refuses to trust him has long since been under the death sentence without knowing it.

And why? Because of that person's failure to believe in Jesus, Son of God when introduced to Him. (John 3:16–18 The Message)

5

The Perseverance that Led to a Miracle

College days in Madras had some days worth remembering. They used to call me "Sam." My first name was "Jeyachandran" and so short for "Samuel" was more effortless. Whenever I played ground hockey or ran long-distance track events, they would shout, "Go, Sam!"

During my intense five-year architectural program in college, my involvement in sports proved to be more than I bargained for, but it was incredible. I started running 800 meters, 1,500, and 3,000-meter races as well as other track events. It was even great to have been selected for the ground hockey team in the first year.

My college was fifteen miles from home. So riding my bike to classes was a thirty-mile roundtrip that seemed long, but it seemed better than taking two buses and a train to get to my college each way. But sometimes, when it reaches over 105 degrees Fahrenheit and close to 100 percent humidity, it was tough peddling when you are sweating even though the wind was blowing against you. But through it all, I kept biking quite a bit during my five years in college, and I was building stamina without realizing it.

In my fourth year of college, one of my friends suggested that I enter the bike race. I laughed and pointed out that my bike was only a one-speed bike and that most of the guys in the race would have new ten-speed bikes. It was out of the question.

My answer to my friends was, "How could I compete with the guys with ten-speeds?" One of my friends kept insisting that I should enter anyway. I told him that I would think about it. After a few days, I decided to enter the race.

So on the day of the race, I showed up and registered. Our college bike race was unusual. It was held on the eight-hundred-meter college track requiring thirty laps to the finish line. I wondered how I could ever compete in such a long race. So my plan was this. I would do my best to keep a good speed and go as much distance as before tiring out. Having only experienced the course only on my foot and never on my bike, I was unsure what speed to go at the start. I decided to go full throttle.

The race started. I sprang out of the starting line at full speed and started leading the whole gang. There must have been about forty to fifty competitors in the bike race. After the third and fourth lap, my lead in the race was huge. Everyone else was pacing themselves for the long race. The guy holding the loudspeaker was one of my friends. He started shouting in the microphone, "Sam, slow down, slow down, you have got twenty-six more rounds." That didn't bother me. I just kept going full speed.

Next round, more of my friends were shouting for me to slow down. Since we were going around the track, I started noticing others getting off their bikes with flat tires, chains coming off their wheels, and all sorts of problems. But that didn't bother me; I was going full throttle, never minding the others.

But my focus was on the end of the race. By God's grace, I was able to finish the whole course, taking first place. I never expected I would finish, especially to come in first. It was astounding that on my first try, I had won the race. Everybody was totally amazed, just like I was.

I realized that all the years of biking thirty miles each day had built my stamina and endurance over the years. When I started to bike to my college and back, it was hard, especially on the hot, humid days of Madras, but I just kept pedaling. It paid off. When I first entered the race, no one even noticed me because an unknown had entered the race, but not at the end.

In my fifth and final year, I entered again, and this time, my friend offered me his ten-speed bike. I won that year also. Those days were hard to forget. To me, these were miracles from God that I least expected.

I learned perseverance and my will, played so much in what I did. Every time I got a negative thought or doubt, I didn't give in. When I committed my negative thoughts to Jesus, as the Bible says below, "I can do all things through Christ who gives me strength" (Philippians 4:13 BSB).

I can do all things I never even dreamed of because Jesus is always with me! So many verses in the Bible can help me persevere to quiet all the voices of doubt and uncertainty! But consider the following verses from the Bible.

> *Do you not know that in a race all the runners run, but only one gets the prize? Run in such a way as to get the prize. Everyone who competes in the games goes into strict training. They do it to get a crown that will not last, but we do it to get a crown that will last forever.* (1 Corinthians 9:24–25 NIV)

> Jesus said: *"For what use is it to gain all the wealth and power of this world, with everything it could offer you, at the cost of your own life?"* (Mark 8:36, Passion)

6

Calculus Was Not My Cup of Tea

My architectural program was five years. Each year had three semesters. Then we had the summer holidays. But two summers were reserved for two internships. Between the second and third year, summer was one of those internships.

I had been assigned to the new building that was under construction and was a fifteen-story office tower. It was the LIC building, one of the tallest at that time in Madras. I was assigned each week to supervise one part of the construction. There were ten weeks I had to be there and watch ten different subtrades. The building was of concrete and steel, and I was learning in classes; it gave me a great introduction to construction.

One week, I watched how they were casting pre-cast concrete slabs. Next week, how they placed windows on the exterior walls. Another week, the plumbing—another, electrical wiring. One of the weeks, I was placed on the roof to watch how roofing was getting done. Madras gets very hot between 105 to 108 degrees and close to 100 percent humidity in the summer (my remembrance), and being on top of the fifteenth floor, was becoming unbearable; plus, this roof was a tar and gravel roof.

They had to heat the tar and evenly spread it on the roof. But to apply tar, they had to heat it to high heat and then spread it. It is adding fuel to the fire. I was getting roasted on the roof when I was watching them do the work.

One day, as I stood there watching them heat the tar and spread it on the roof, this older man came and asked me why I was there in the hot sun watching them work. I told him I was an architectural student, and watching them do the roofing was part of my studies.

Then he told me how he never got to study when he was a student, and even though his parents had sent him to school, he was never studious. He wasted his time. He told me almost as a warning that when I was given the privilege to study, I should do my best to do well at school, so I don't have to work in the hot sun, heating tar on top of roofs like he was.

That was a precious lesson for me. I was not a very happy camper on top of a fifteen-story building under the hot sun, watching them pour hot tar. So would I do that as my vocation? As the man said, he was doing it because he wasted his time at school, when he was supposed to study. That spoke volumes to me that I better be diligent in my studies when my parents gave me the privilege to learn rather than wasting it.

Math wasn't my favorite subject. The first year, I had to take Calculus. Calculus wasn't my cup of tea. And I was having difficulty. I asked my classmates why we have to take Math if we are designing buildings. The answer came: we need to have structural engineering to calculate simple structures and not use a consultant. The following year, we were into Structural Engineering to design bridges and high-rise buildings. My question to my classmates, we may never design bridges and high-rise buildings. The answer came, no questions asked, do what the professor says.

So even as these questions came, the thought came from what the older man said on the roof, I better study given the privilege and not waste my time. So even though, it seemed like a bitter pill, I had to work hard to study

Calculus and Structural Engineering. If I do well, I don't have to toil in the hot sun on the roof, as he did.

I remembered a verse in the Bible: "Study to show yourself unto God, a workman that need not to be ashamed, rightly dividing the Word of Truth" (2 Timothy 2:15 NIV).

It is through our study of God's Word that we substantiate that we are already accepted in Christ, as in Ephesians 1:6, "Wherein God has predestined me to be adopted as His son,...to the praise of his glorious grace that he lavished on us in the Beloved One, Jesus," that God calls me as His son. Yes, God calls me His adopted son. Unless I take the time to study God's Word, I will not be made aware of all His promises for me. Look what 3 John 2 says, "Beloved, I pray that in every way you may succeed and prosper and be in good health, physically, just as I know, your soul prospers spiritually."

God wants me to succeed and prosper and be in good health, even as I take the time to study God's Word, that my soul prospers spiritually in God. It may not be my cup of tea, but I don't want to miss out on all His promises. I had to repent of my foolish ways; I needed to study, make every effort, ponder on His Word as much as possible to get His blessings. Now that I have made up my mind to study His Word for at least one hour every day, to read, to ponder, to get the Holy Spirit's revelations more and more each day. I use different translations, write them down, memorize them, use His Word as my prayers to Him, slice it and dice it so that I can chew on His words, so many nuggets, I find along the way. He makes all things possible for my life to prosper and succeed and be in good health even as I spend time as much as I can, studying God's Word now, even as God calls me His adopted son. He loves me, yea, yea, yea! What privilege, what great News as I live in His blessing!

7

Christmas in India

Christmas in India was quite different from Christmas in the US as far as I can remember. I left India when I was twenty-four. But the memories of those early years in India are still vivid in my mind. I can remember as early as when I was four years old. It may not be entirely accurate, but I'll write what I remember as my memories come back.

I was brought up in the Anglican church. With it being part of a Protestant church, some of the early church traditions became more traditional. They vary from church to church and from place to place, but all the prayers and hymns were all true to the gospel even though sometimes we tend to repeat the prayers without meaning them or take them as part of our hearts and lives.

As early as four years old, I remember being part of the choir and walking in the middle of the aisle, being part of the procession from the back of the church to the altar in the front. I believe that at times, I led the procession, carrying a cross. This happened at All Saints Church in Trichy, South India.

I remember that during the latter part of November and December, there were so many carols and Christmas music; we were immersed in them. Even though the population of Trichy is close to a million now, when I grew up there, it may have been half the size. There were many churches, and almost all of them had choirs. And all the choirs would go out carol singing four or five times during the season. They would start after dinner in the evening and travel to many homes. They would stop, go into the house, and sing two or three carols in each home. Then the Christmas story would be read from the Bible. This they did till about 3:00 or 4:00 a.m.

I remember one year when my dad had arranged for a large open truck and filled it with our choir from our church along with musical instruments like violins, guitars, and even a portable organ. He took us all to a fancy restaurant of his friend's and gave us an outstanding dinner before setting out to visit the homes. We had sent postcards to all the homes we were to see, telling them that we would be coming to their homes at a specific time of the night. Usually, they would prepare appetizers, sweets, and snacks and wait for us to come. Then we visited each home, starting with singing a carol in front of the house. If it was after 11:00 p.m., that carol singing would wake them if they had gone to sleep. After a carol at the front, they would invite us in, we'd sing another carol or two, and they'd offer us sweets and snacks to eat. Some in the choir would usually know someone at the home, and they would greet each other and talk.

But since we had a great dinner to start with on that night, we were able to eat in only the first two or three houses, and afterward, we were so full that we could not eat anymore. They were disappointed that we would not eat anything they had prepared for us. But they enjoyed the music we sang. Those were the days I look back on and treasure.

But with the singing and visiting with the church members, we had a great time. Then other churches would visit us as well. In between, there were other Christmas services that we would attend.

Even as I grew older, I always looked forward to December. Even on the days that I had not gone caroling, I looked for the days that carolers would visit us. We must have sung so many times, but we still never got tired.

O Come All Ye faithful, joyful and triumphant,
O come ye to Bethlehem,
Come and behold Him,
Born the King of Angels;
O come, let us adore Him,
Christ the Lord.

These are beautiful days to remember. They was so much worshipful music, so much celebration that Jesus was born.

Year after year, December would come, and Christmas filled our lives. We moved to Madras, a much bigger town. There were more churches, and this intensity even increased. Christmas day was also different there. On Christmas day, the church service was at 4:30 a.m. So we would get up at 3:00 a.m., and I would put on my new shirt and pants and sometimes new shoes. We'd get dressed and left for church. Some of the streets were dark, and no one was on the roads. But the church was fully lit up. We got to sing carols, and sometimes it was Handel's Messiah. But Christmas day was the last day that we sang carols.

We never exchanged gifts like people do here, but we'd have a great breakfast and a great lunch. It was a day to make merry and celebrate the birthday of Jesus. It was full of happy memories.

The Christmas story was so unique. The uncle of Jesus was a high priest. Yet when the angel appeared, he questioned him, "How will I be certain of this?" So for nine months, he could not speak. So when John was born, finally, he was able to talk and enjoy a new son. The angel also appeared to Joseph, and Joseph did what he was told. Then the angel appeared to Mary and said to her that she would have a baby; she told him, "Let it be to me according to your word."

This is the greatest news ever told. It is the greatest birth and the most celebrated one. The Greatest One was born, and the prophecy that was prophesied seven hundred years before by Isaiah, the Jewish prophet of Jesus of Nazareth, came true.

> *For unto us a Child is born,*
> *Unto us a Son is given;*

And the government will be upon His shoulder.
And His name will be called
Wonderful, Counselor, Mighty God,
Everlasting Father, Prince of Peace. Isaiah 9:6 (NKJV)

8

The Amazing Parallels

My friend was curious. I was telling him about my travels.

"So you left Madras, India, went to London, then to Calgary, Vancouver, New York, and finally Los Angeles? Six cities in six years?" he asked.

"Yes, till I came to Los Angeles."

"So tell me, before you left, how was your life in Madras?"

"In Madras, I was staying with my parents till I left for London. So it was a nice house with a big yard. Interestingly, we were in the heart of a city with ten million, yet have a compound with land over 10,000 square feet. We had a chicken coup of about thirty birds as well as turkey at times. So they provided us eggs every day and chicken when we needed them for dinner."

"That's so cool. Chicken coup in your backyard!"

"I have also seen chickens running with their heads cut off!"

"Yek! What did your dad do?"

"My dad was the director of Animal Husbandry for the State of Madras, and since it was a government job, he was provided with a driver, a servant, and a gardener."

"Did you stay at home till you left abroad?"

"Yes, I did, except for one year I stayed at our college dorm. College was fifteen miles away. I biked every day, quite a bit of the time. But in my last year, I stayed in the dorm. Then I moved back after I graduated. I loved staying at home. My dad was very strict, but since I had four older sisters, they spoilt me. Even though we didn't have cell phones, I had many friends and cousins who kept visiting me."

"So if you had a comfortable life, what made you leave India?"

"Good question. When I was doing undergrad architecture, I loved modern architecture in the US. I wanted to continue and do graduate work. None was available locally in Madras. One thing led to another, and the only way to do that was to travel abroad and study."

"Did everything work out for you to leave?"

"Are you kidding? It was tough. Many times, I wanted to give up. And at times, it seemed everything fell into place. After I graduated with my bachelor's in architecture, I applied to two universities in the US and got into both. One of them even gave me a full assistantship, and I was overjoyed. Then a month later, they canceled, and what a letdown that was."

"I can see that. They give it to you and then take it away. Bummer!"

"I didn't have the funds to pay fees and living expenses. Then a friend in Madras, Bob Butts from Calgary, Canada, asked me why can't I work and study there. He asked me to give my resume to him, and then he sent it to his sponsor, Ray Stevens. His sponsor then mailed it to all the architects in Calgary. Then I got a job offer from a large firm, and I decided to take it."

"If you decided to go to Calgary, why did you stay in London?"

"When I wanted to get a work visa to Canada, I found out it took more than a year to get a visa in India but only about two months from London for Canada. I didn't think the firm that offered me will wait for a year. Since I had a professional degree and two years' work experience, I could only get a work visa to London in two weeks. I asked the firm in Calgary if they would wait, and they agreed. So I decided to go to London and get a visa there for Canada."

"Wow! It looks like that worked out!"

"Not quite. As I was getting ready for the trip, I found out I can only take out $10 from India."

"How did you manage with that?"

"Stand up on my head! My dad had arranged for me to stay at Indian YMCA for a month without paying. They served breakfast and dinner as part of the stay. So I was the last to have breakfast at the dining hall and the first one for dinner. In the middle, I starved. But it was God's amazing grace that kept me going. Even though I was so lonely at times, God's presence held me together even at tough times!"

"Still, practically, how did you manage with $10 for the first month?"

"What $10? Yes, I did leave Madras with $10. I had to change planes in Rome, and when I got back to the airport in Rome, the authorities charged $5, so when I landed in London, I had $5. Then I had to pay $2 for bus fare from the airport to YMCA. So I was left with $3."

"Tough situation, only $3, to fend for yourself?"

"By the way, when I landed in London, I didn't have a job. So I converted my $3 to pennies and shillings. After that, I looked at all the ads in newspapers at YMCA, and I would use the pennies to make calls for the ads. I walked for all my job interviews. I was very frugal with my money."

"Did you regret being in such a tough place?"

"No. I knew God was with me. All through the process, even in Madras, I just leaned on God to lead my way. So even though I was lonely and homesick, I just hung on to God. I took Jesus at His Word, who said He will never leave me nor forsake me and trusted Him."

"Brave man."

"I had my Bible with me and kept reading and meditating. As I was reading about Abraham, when God asked him to leave his family and go where God wanted him to go, Bible says he never looked back at the comforts of where he was. He was a great example for me! So leaving a nice home to a small eight feet by nine feet room in at the Indian YMCA, London. It was so different, but I never looked back at the comforts of my house in Madras."

"Did you know you were moving again every time you landed in a city?"

"No, except in London," I replied.

"How come only at London?"

"I was in London only three months, only to get a quicker visa to Canada, where I had an offer for work. But I had only two pounds when I landed in England, and I didn't have any promise of work either."

"That's amazing. So even though you landed in London only with less than two British pounds, you were able to go to Calgary in three months?"

"Yes, indeed."

"But how? It looks like a miracle or the Queen helped you."

"It was more on the miraculous side."

"Must be a fascinating story. Can you tell me the whole story now or at another time?" He seemed to plead.

"I wrote a whole chapter of getting to London and my getting work in London, and I will give it to you. You can read it on your own time."

"Okay, how about the other cities?"

"I have to write about Calgary and Vancouver."

"When you landed in Calgary, did you think you were going to stay?"

"Yes, indeed I did."

"What was the twist that happened? You left Calgary?"

"The purpose of my going to Calgary was to do my graduate degree even though I had an offer of a job there. So I stayed with Steven's family in Calgary and joined work. Ray Stevens was the sponsor for Bob, my friend in Madras. But then I found out, the University of Calgary didn't have a graduate program in architecture."

"Yes, each step was not as expected, haha! That's why you left."

"Let me read verses from the Bible. 'By faith, Abraham obeyed when he was called to go out to the place which he would receive as an inheritance. And he went out, not knowing where he was going. By faith, he dwelt in the land of promise as *in* a foreign country, dwelling in tents, for he waited for the city which has foundations, whose builder and maker *is* God.'" I read the Bible passage to him.

"So are you saying, you came to Calgary and found out, they didn't have a program that you came for, it was like, 'not knowing where you were going'?"

"Yes, I was discouraged first, but then I knew God had a purpose in all my travels. At the University of Calgary, they advised me to go to Vancouver, and there at University of British Columbia, they had a graduate program in architecture."

"I see your point. So you had to move to Vancouver, and to you, it was like everywhere you moved, it was like you were living in a tent."

"Exactly, it seemed as if I didn't know where I was going, moved from Madras to London, London to Calgary, and now I have to move to Vancouver, and still I haven't started my graduate studies."

"Interesting. Couldn't you have found out in Madras, there was no graduate program in Calgary and gone straight to Vancouver?"

"Sorry, they didn't have google those days, just joking. Remember, I had an offer for a job in Calgary, so I had to land in Calgary. And Ray Stevens was there in Calgary. And it was a bridge for me to get into North America. And also, when I left with only $10, I didn't have too many choices."

"Very true, but you got to see London, staying there for about three months, see Calgary, staying there for a year, and now you were going to Vancouver."

"Yes, indeed. I hardly had any money to start with. God made that all possible. I was a bachelor, and I didn't have to worry about a family. I depended on God like Abraham, and He made all my travel plans."

"Yes, living from tent to tent, till you arrived at the city which had foundations or a graduate program."

"I didn't know what the next day held for me. But I knew God was with me. I had trusted Him, and even though I was lonely, I knew He wouldn't let me down."

My friend said, "Not knowing where you were going was a parallel for you. Another verse, Hebrews 11:1, 'Now faith is the substance of things hoped for, the evidence of things not seen.' I knew you wanted to study for your Masters and hoped for it, but you didn't see any evidence of how you would do it. You had the faith for what you left India for, with $10, hoped to study, even though you didn't have any evidence to see."

"Yes, very true. I was only taking one step at a time. So after I decided to go to Vancouver, I left my job in Calgary, put all my things in the back of my car, left for Vancouver with a friend. I found an apartment in Vancouver, and I also found a job to support myself. After being in Vancouver for only about two weeks, there was a knock on my door. Ray Steven showed up, saying he received a telegram from my mom that my dad had passed away. That was very sad."

"Yes, very sad. How did you take it?"

"Not very good. Good thing Ray Stevens was there for me to cry over his shoulder. In Calgary, he was like my father to me, loving and supporting me in all that I did. So was his church in Calgary—very loving indeed. Great times of friendships for sometimes, my lonely days. But I had to move on."

"So what happened to your Graduate program in Vancouver?"

"I found that I can take a few units in the University of British Columbia, called UBC, and I started taking evening classes while working full time. But after six months, I found out forty hours of work and three evenings of classes was too much for me. So I decided I will save up money and go full time to do my Master's. So I was very frugal with my funds, saving for my studies."

"So how long did it take?"

"I was in Vancouver for two years and was able to save all I needed. I applied to Pratt Institute, a very old Architectural School founded in 1887, known for architects in New York, and to the University of Oregon. I went to Eugene, Oregon, by train, for an interview. And Pratt, the head of the Graduate Program, called me by phone and had an interview. And Pratt accepted me right away, and I accepted it, knowing it was a great School of Architecture, one of the ten best in the US."

"How did the money part work out?"

"Yes, it was a one-year Master's program. Adding the fees and all the living costs in Pratt's brochure worked out as long as I sold my car and found a place to live as had been projected. So it again took faith to go one year of studies without working to support me. Again I felt like Abraham, took faith in quitting my job in Vancouver and moving to New York."

"Were you apprehensive?"

"Not really. I left Madras with $10, left London with $60, and left Calgary with more, but now I had saved much more, paid for all of Pratt's fees, and a year of living expenses. I had trusted God so long that now it was easier, knowing He was going with me."

"Wow! You were able to save that much?"

"After I decided that I was going to college full time, I was so frugal. I discarded my credit cards and bank account except for a savings account. I paid everything in cash, which made me count every penny I spent. So I was surprised myself how much I was able to save. When I focused like what Abraham did, he was counting the stars and counting the sand, so I did count my pennies."

"That's great! So how did it go in New York?"

"Went very well. I was able to get a room with two other undergraduate students, next block to the campus. The first day of classes began. I was surprised to see one of my classmates from my bachelor's course in Madras in the same program. I liked all my classmates and enjoyed all my lecturers and professors. Most of them were great architects in New York. There was a famous Architectural History professor that would pack the class, so one has to get there a half hour before to get a seat."

"So you enjoyed your time there?"

"Yes, indeed. I would go to New York City with my roommates or classmates and enjoy seeing all the great buildings and the great boulevards. At times, we would get free tickets for Broadway plays, Philharmonic Orchestra Concerts, Ballet, and many more at the student centers. After a couple of months of a fun time, it was time to study. Yes, it was great going to Pratt. I enjoyed it."

"So did you finish your master's in one year, as you planned?"

"I finished all my course work taking eighteen units per semester in one year, but I could not finish my thesis. So my professor said I could be working, and he will meet me on Saturdays to review my progress. So that's what I did. I found a great job in New York and finished my thesis in less than six months, and I got my master's."

"That's great. So what have you learned over the years?"

"When I was reading Mark chapter 6, Jesus took five loaves and two fish and multiplied them to feed five thousand men plus women and kids. He took my measly $10 and multiplied them even when I was jumping from country to country, even graduating from a graduate school. It was a miracle. That chapter went on to say, everyone ate and was satisfied, and so was I. The key to multiplication was to have coffee with Jesus every morning and meditating on His Word. Every day, at least for an hour, I do that, and He keeps multiplying miracles every day. Amazing!"

"Yes, now that I have heard your story, I need to brush up on Abraham's story, so many chapters in Genesis, as well as Jesus, multiplying two fish and five loaves to feed the five thousand men plus the women and the children as well.

Miracles just didn't happen in Jesus's day, but after hearing your story, they are happening even now!"

"Yes, I agree. I say, 'Amen to that!'"

9

Calgary to Montana

I had gone to Calgary looking to do my graduate program, but I found no graduate program at the University of Calgary after I got there. Since, I was offered a job when I was in India, I took the job and stayed there for a year. I got involved with the youth program at the local church and got excellent friends. A long weekend came up, and two of my friends wanted to go out somewhere for three days. Montana was not very far, and so we planned a trip for three days.

I have never been to the US, and since I had a Canadian work permit, it was okay for me to visit the US. One of my friends decided to drive his car, and I went along for the ride. One was Reggie and the other was Tom. We looked at the map and planned where we were going to go and come back. Finally, the day arrived, and we left according to my friends' plan. Shortly we were in Montana, and we started climbing into the Montana mountains.

It was amazing. Even as we climbed up the mountains, we suddenly drove on a four-lane freeway, about ten thousand–plus feet in elevation. It seemed to be on top of the world, with incredible sceneries even as we were moving along. Glad I was not driving, so my eyes were glued to the heavenly scenery all around me. We were close to Glacier National Park. I was spellbound even as I gazed in where we were. I thoroughly enjoyed the beauty of the world we live in, and it was like being in heaven on earth.

We were headed to Great Falls, Montana, and since my friends had planned the trip, I went along for the ride, but what a ride it was, I had never seen anything like it before. It was so long ago, but these sceneries still stick to my mind. My friends told me that we should look for where the great falls are, and hopefully, we can even get under the falls. Coming from India, I told them that I didn't want to get under the chilly waters and shiver.

We did get to the city, and we didn't see any signs of the great falls. So we parked the car downtown and asked around how to head to the falls. Some of them were bewildered. One of them said there are no falls here; this is only a town with a name, but there were no falls. We were very disappointed. We thought we were driving all the way to see these great falls but nothing.

For me, it was still worth going through all the heavenly scenery. Then we headed to Butte, Bozeman, and Billings. Billings was one of the most significant towns in the area, and again, we parked our car downtown and walked around. My friend started taking pictures of a cop. I asked him what was so great about him. He said in Canada, we never see a cop with a gun, but in the US, they wear the gun in a sling-like in the Western movies, and it amazed him to see.

As we walked around downtown, I saw a guitar and amplifier with a price tag in the window of a music store. So I looked at the price tags and called my friends.

I said, "Look, these prices are ridiculously low!"

They said, "Yes, US prices are way below what we pay in Canada."

I replied, "You know I have a guitar, but I would love to buy that amplifier to go with my guitar!"

They said, "Let's go inside and check it out."

So we went in and asked a salesman if we can check out the amplifier. The salesman bought a guitar as well and turned on the amplifier. He also gave me the guitar to check it out. So I played, and it sounded good, and then I asked the salesman, "I need only the amplifier, and can you just sell me the amplifier?"

He said, "Yes, we can just sell you the amplifier."

I asked Reggie, "Can I buy this, and would there be room in your car?"

"Yes, no problem. We will make room."

I was happy that I got such a good deal, and I was able to take it back with me.

After few hours, we decided to head back to Calgary. On the way, Tom asked me, "Jey, do you have money to pay customs duty if, on the border, they ask you for it?"

I replied, "What custom duty?"

He replied, "Canadian Customs may ask you to pay because you are bringing in what was made in the US."

"Wow!" I replied. "I did know that. Is that true? I spent all the money I had on that amplifier."

"They may ask you, or they may not. It depends on what item it is and how much it costs. I don't know what to say, especially if you don't have any money left."

Reggie said, "Everything happened in a hurry, that none of us thought of this before you bought this. We are all students, so we are in this together with you. Now before we cross the border, we need to think before we go through."

There was silence for a while. Then one of my friends spoke up and said, "Jey, as I was thinking, these thoughts came to my mind, whether it is legal or not, and we don't want you to get in trouble. But my suggestion is to place the amplifier behind the front seat and in the car's legroom. Then we will put some blankets we have over it to hide it. Then one of you sleeps over it. Then we cross the border. The security guard may see you sleeping and may not ask you to get up, so he will never see the amplifier."

Then there was more silence. Then Tom said, "Okay, that sounds like a plan. Let me sleep over it, and the guard may notice that I am a Canadian and may not ask me to get up. Because you are from India, he may want to question you. That's okay with me."

So we all agreed. We stopped the car, moved stuff around as we talked, and took off again. As we got close to the border, my friend went to sleep over the blankets and the amplifier in the back. Everything went as we planned, and the border guard never asked many questions. He wanted to see my passport, and he saw my passport with my Canadian work visa stamped on it and let us go. Then after we passed the border, we all shouted for joy with the guilty look on our faces. We felt terrible for what we did, but even through that ordeal, it worked out fine. This reminded me of the story from the TV show *Hogan's Heroes* where the American prisoners kept planning their schemes over the German soldiers.

But I had to repent before the Lord for what I had done. It reminded these verses below.

If we say that we have fellowship with Him, and walk in darkness, we lie and do not practice the truth. But if we walk in the

*light as He is in the light, we have fellow-
ship with one another, and the blood of Jesus
Christ His Son cleanses us from all sin.*

*If we say that we have no sin, we deceive
ourselves, and the truth is not in us. If we
confess our sins, He is faithful and just to
forgive us our sins and to cleanse us from all
unrighteousness. If we say that we have not
sinned, we make Him a liar, and His Word
is not in us.* (1 John 1:8–10 NKJV)

Yes, since I repented, I know I am forgiven. I know
what I did was wrong. I know Jesus died to pay my punishment for the wrong I did. I have confessed it, and now I
am forgiven. His Word says that He is faithful and just to
forgive my sins and cleanse me from all unrighteousness.
Something I learned was Jesus's love for me when I have
fellowship with Him. I do silly things in the heat of the
moment, but I can always take it to my Lord. He has so
much love for me that even when I fall into doing wrong
and try to hide it when I confess them to Him, He is faithful to forgive me because He took my sins on the cross
where He was crucified for me. How I am grateful for His
love and tenderness and mercy!

Oh, the love that sought me!
Oh, the love that bought me!
Oh, the grace that brought me to the flock!
Wondrous grace that brought me to the
flock!

10

Woven Together for Good

Having saved enough funds to go to graduate school full time, I landed at Pratt Institute in New York, a 130-year-old architecture school. Some of the best architects from New York City teach there, so I was thrilled to go. I loved the school and loved the city.

I got into the right classes and was also able to move into an apartment with two other fourth-year students, Chuck and Ted. It was within a block of the school, just the proper distance. Since my roommates had been there for years, they had a whole bunch of friends. And I loved hanging out with my new roommates and their friends.

Most of our classes were between 8:00 a.m. and 1:00 p.m.; that seemed the same for my roommates. So we would all come back after classes, and all their friends would show up. It was visiting time all afternoon, having conversations with lots of laughter and jokes. It was hard not to join in.

Also, at our campus, they were giving out free tickets to both Broadway and off-Broadway shows, to Lincoln Center, Operas, Philharmonic's, and everything New York had to offer. We went to many of them and enjoyed all the free tickets and shows.

But that was the problem. We were hanging out instead of studying. The studies seemed to have taken a back seat. A month went by, and then another month. Realizing that my dream was to do graduate work and the three years I had saved funds to do it was draining away, I faced my roommates.

I told them, "Hey, guys, it has been great fun the last two months staying with you. But I haven't done much studying these days. How long can we waste time like this?"

Chuck replied, "Jey, I was thinking the same. Somehow everyone walks into our place, and they never seem to leave. In the end, we get the raw deal. No time for studies. What are we going to do?"

Ted said, "I agree. We have to do something drastic. My dad won't be a happy camper if he looks at my grades. We need to make up our mind and change our behavior."

"Yes, I'm ready. Whatever it takes," I said.

Chuck said, "I have an idea, but you guys may not like it. But I'm game. We need to make up our mind and stick to it—no going back."

"I'm ready to listen. What's the plan?"

Ted agreed, "Spit it out, Chuck."

"This is the plan. All of us come back from classes around 1:00 p.m. We place a sign on the door, 'Do not disturb.' Once we get in, we don't open our door, no matter how loud the knocking. You can check the answering machines but no returning calls unless it's an emergency. We'll all get a quick bite to eat—sandwiches. Turn off all phones. Then we all get a nap. Sleep till about 5:00 or 5:30 p.m., get up, have coffee, and then study or do assignments. Then around 7:30 or 8:00 p.m., cook and have dinner and then study all night."

"Are you crazy?" Ted said. "Did you just come from Mars? Don't you need to sleep? Just a nap would do for you?"

Chuck replied, "Hey, Ted, you wanted to do something drastic, and this is it. Yes, it will take a few days to work in our system, like jetlag. But think of it, how many hours do you get to study per day now? If I get at least two hours now, that'll be good. But with my plan, you can easily get to study eight to ten hours. I also suggest that every one or two hours at night, we all get together and have coffee or snacks to check up on each other, so no one goes to sleep on the books."

I commented, "Eight to ten hours. Chuck, that'll be great. I can get a lot of studying done. I can also spend more time on my designs, and my professor would like it. Let's do it."

Ted chuckled. "You guys have convinced me. I'm ready to take the plunge. I hope, in the end, my dad will like the grades I get."

Chuck grinned. "Is it a pact? Have we all made up our minds? We're all in it together, understand? It's sink or swim, buddies!"

I echoed, "Yes, we're all in it together. Made up our minds. Yes, Ted, what is your final answer?"

Ted replied, "My final answer…yes. Count me in. Now I have to tell all my friends our plans. They'll think we're crazy."

"Why do you have to tell your friends now?"

Ted answered, "If I don't, they'll keep knocking on our doors till our ears pop out. I'm telling you, till we all let the whole world know, they'll all be bugging us. But when I get my good grades, they'll be jealous."

Chuck said, "Ted's got a good point. I need to tell my friends as well. We'll start our new plan tomorrow. See how it goes. I'm glad you all agreed."

Yes, our plan went well. It was hard for me to stay awake past the midnight hour the first few days, but slowly I stayed up studying. The pleasures of staying up late had unusual moments. We were on the fifth floor, and I had a balcony. One night at 3:00 a.m., I heard gunshots. I went over to the balcony and saw a sight I could only see in New York, and I called my roommates to watch as well.

A lone gunman was chasing another guy, trying to shoot him in the back. Gunshots rang out. They were running so fast, and I didn't know the gunman ever hit the other. Then they both disappeared into the darkness.

Another night, at 4:00 a.m., we heard a lot of commotion down below, and we rushed down to the lobby to find a crowd staring at a man bleeding to death. The story was that three guys were trying to change a tire at 3:00 a.m. in our parking lot, and this guy walked by. The three called him to help them, to which he replied he was too tired and going to bed. Since he wouldn't help them, the three beat him up with the tire iron and left him bleeding.

Many other episodes happened that could only occur after midnight that I can't fill my book with. Oh, the joys of staying up. Only in New York could they take place.

During Christmas vacation, I asked the school permission to work in an architect's office. They granted my request, and I found a job in Lower Manhattan.

I reported to work on a Monday when my winter break began. The first morning went well. But 2:00 p.m. came; there was a knock on my head. Yes, on my head.

"Jey, Jey, wake up. What are you doing sleeping on the drafting table?"

That was my boss who found me fast asleep at work. I woke up kind of in a daze. Part of our pattern to study was to sleep in the afternoons. Now that pattern came back to bite me.

"Mr. Jacobs, I'm so sorry. I have been studying for the graduate program by staying up all night long but sleeping in the afternoons. I've been doing that for the last two months. I apologize. I won't do it again." I stammered my words out.

"No excuses. Make sure it doesn't happen again," he said.

"Yes, sir," I told him.

By making up our minds early on, we reaped the benefits. I was thrilled to receive a 3.9 GPA when I graduated. If I had not done one of the subjects poorly, in the beginning, I would have received a 4.0. Still, it was great. I enjoyed too much of New York in the beginning.

But God was good. He made my dream come true upon my graduation. All the sleepless nights paid off, and I was so glad I had made up my mind to study. I never regretted the decision I made.

"So we are convinced that every detail of our lives is continually woven together for good for we are God's lovers who have been called to fulfill His designed purpose" (Romans 8:28 Passion).

11

New York to Los Angeles!

New York was fun initially, but after I started working there, the commute to work was terrible, not to mention the weather. June came, and it was hot and muggy after a cold, snowy winter. The pay was good, but I was getting tired of living there. I was working full-time and doing my thesis at the same time. But after the hot summer, I faced the winter again. I didn't look forward to another winter.

So as I was getting close to finishing my thesis, I thought about whether I should remain in New York or move somewhere else. I was a bachelor, and I made up my mind; the question was "Where?" When I lived in Calgary, Ray Stevens and his family always went somewhere in Los Angeles for the winter break, and they used to tell me how beautiful the weather was in the winter. They always looked forward to going there after Christmas.

Then I found out one of my classmates in my college days in India lived in Tustin, south of Los Angeles. So I was able to get his phone number, and I called him. I asked him whether I could go there and stay for a few days with him. And he said, by all means, that it was okay to stay with him for as long as I wanted. I asked him about jobs, and he said it was easy to get them.

So I finished my thesis and got my degree in January. And as soon as I got my degree, I gave a notice at my job and informed them where I was staying. Then I left for LA along with a friend.

We planned to travel for a week, doing some sightseeing on the way. We planned to stay in Pittsburgh with a friend of mine. So we left. And as we approached the city, we caught this weird smell like rotten eggs. I thought something had gone wrong with my car engine, so I stopped and opened the hood. But it was not my car; this smell was in the air.

So when we saw my friend who lived there, I asked him about the smell, and he told me it was coming from all the steel mills. There were so many steel mills there, and they polluted the river. I guess all that lived there got used to the smell as well as the pollution.

We kept driving, arrived at Indianapolis, and stopped at a fast-food place to get lunch. Everyone spoke in such a heavy Southern accent, and we were amazed and had a hard time understanding them. But now, things have changed. Pittsburgh does not have the smell anymore, and the Southern accent is almost gone even in the South.

I didn't realize January was still in the middle of winter and that it could snow anytime, but that's what happened when we were about halfway there. We were in Southern Illinois when the snow started to come down pretty heavily, and suddenly everything turned white. And it kept snowing for quite a while. It was also turning to evening, and the sun was setting.

Snow came so heavily that I could barely see what was in front of me as I was driving. Suddenly I saw a massive truck so close in front of me, and I got in a panic and pushed my brakes very hard. We went for a spin two or three times on the freeway the next thing I knew. It was a good thing it was a divided freeway. We landed in the greenbelt in the middle of the divided freeway and stopped. We sat there for about ten minutes in a state of shock. But at that, I knew God was with us there too. Jesus said, "I will never leave, nor forsake you." We were so thankful to Him for saving us and keeping us alive, safe, and sound.

There, while we were spinning on the icy freeway, we never hit anything and then landed in a muddy grass divider, and then the mud acted as a cushion—a miraculous landing pad. That was a miracle indeed, and only God could have saved us. So after ten minutes, we tried to open the doors, but they would not open. We pushed to open, but no, it wouldn't open. The car had gone so deep into the mud. We couldn't see out of the windows either since the snow was still coming down so hard. It was slushy snow.

So we had to roll our windows down and then climb out and drop down on mud. It was pitch-black dark when we got out. Our feet were going into the mud, so getting back on the freeway pavement was quite a task. We could see cars going slower because of the heavy snow. But other than cars and trucks, we could not see any light anywhere in the dark.

We did not know which way to walk for help or see any town. As we walked a little further, we saw a tiny speckle of light far away. So we started walking toward that light and found out it was a small town. We saw an auto repair shop, and we thought we could get a tow truck to get our car. It was quite a struggle to pull the car out of the mud and back to the repair shop. We found a motel, and the following day, the repair shop hoisted the vehicle to check for any damages. There were none. The whole thing was a miracle that displayed how God cares for His children. He was there with us through it all even as we faced the stormy snow.

> *When you face stormy seas, I will be there with you with endurance and calm; you will not be engulfed in raging rivers. If it seems like you're walking through fire with flames licking at your limbs, keep going; you won't be burned. Because, I am your God.* (Isaiah 43:2–3 Voice)

We were back on the road again, heading out to California. We took about a week driving to Los Angeles, doing some sightseeing on the way. Everything worked out fine, and I dropped my friend in Los Angeles. Then I landed in my classmate's house in Tustin. It was the first week of February, and it was a sunny, balmy seventy degrees in Tustin. Wow, no more snow but great sunny California weather. I stayed with my classmate for a week. Tustin was in the early stages of development, so there was no appeal to me.

I always wanted to live in San Francisco since many great architects lived there, and after I had seen its pictures, I loved the images of San Francisco before. I decided to leave and look for work there. So I left and looked for work. But in February, it was a rainy season, and it was constantly raining when I was going for interviews and driving. Also, the city had lots of ups and downs, and my car was a stick shift, heavy-duty clutch with wide-wheel tires; I hated driving there. I didn't like the constant rain as well as going up and down on those hills. I decided San Francisco was not the city for me. So I decided to go back to my classmate's home in Tustin, where the weather was excellent even in February.

I went through West Los Angeles, near Beverly Hills and Brentwood, as I was driving back. I saw a sign on the Freeway that said "Sunset Blvd. exit," and I took that exit. I used to watch a TV show called *Sunset Strip*, and there was intrigue on my part. This was in Brentwood, and everything was beautiful. I loved everything that I saw. It was very appealing to me. Beautiful trees, gorgeous big homes— everything was done in such a fancy manner. So I thought, *How about if I see if any architects are looking for a designer?*

I stopped at a store, got a newspaper, and looked through the Wanted ads. There were two ads in the newspaper, and I called both. It was a Friday afternoon, and one architect asked me to come for an interview the following Monday morning. So it was when I was at the interview that the head of the firm offered me a position, and I took it. So I went back to Tustin, picked up all my belongings, and joined work on the next day, Tuesday. *God is so good; He did all things well. Everything He does is wonderful.* It reminded me of another verse:

> *The people were absolutely beside them-*
> *selves and astonished beyond measure. And*
> *they began to say about Jesus, Everything He*
> *does is wonderful!* (Mark 7:37p TPT)

I loved working there. I was mainly designing ski resorts, and even though I wasn't much of a skier, I loved designing the complexes, condos, ski slopes, and whole ski villages. I was working on most of the Colorado, Montana, Idaho, and Utah resorts.

My boss used to attend UCLA and was an Olympic water polo champion, and his best friend's father came from a family that used to own most of Westwood, where UCLA is. The family donated quite a bit of land to UCLA and then sold the rest of Westwood. So my boss's friend became very wealthy, and my boss and his friend both used to be both in the Olympic water polo team together and used to ski together as well. So when his friend got all the wealth, he bought acres of land for ski resorts and told my boss to design them. So that is why I was able to design so many of them. The beach was not that far from my office, but living close to the beach in Santa Monica was expensive.

So as I was looking for a place that I could afford that was close to the beach, I stopped by a Realtor's office. A tall blond guy met me there, and he asked me where I was from, to which I replied, "India."

The next question was "Where in India?"

I replied, "Madras."

Then he spoke in my language, Tamil, and he asked me whether I spoke Tamil—my mother tongue. And I was so taken back because he was fluent in my mother tongue. I was suddenly so taken back. *This Anglo-Saxon guy's speaking in my language.* I was stunned. I found out he was a missionary kid in my part of the country in India, grew up there till he was in high school, and came to the US for college. So he learned

Tamil since he was a kid and spoke it very well. We became good friends, but we did get back to speaking English.

Finally, I did find a place to live. It was in Playa del Rey, and it was a very interesting place. It was upstairs, a lone one-bedroom unit, and from the bedroom, I could see the ocean. Wow, it was such a great unit, and I loved it. But between the unit and the ocean, there was a lake with a lot of ducks. I had windows of three sides of my bedroom: the one to the back, which looked at the ocean, and the two side windows, which looked down at the sand.

On a Saturday morning, I would get up late and look down from my window; there were already people sitting in their bathing suits and kids playing in the sand. God blessed me with such an amazing place to live. I enjoyed every minute in that place. By the way, the weather by the beach was amazing too. Every March and April, I would see cars with the license plates of other states. I figured they all moved here for the weather. As Jackie Gleason used to say, "How sweet it is!" A verse also comes to my mind.

*Every spiritual blessing in the heavenly
realm has already been lavished upon us
as a love gift from our wonderful heavenly*

Father, the Father of our Lord Jesus—all because He sees us wrapped into Christ. This is why we celebrate Him with all our hearts! (Ephesians 1:3 TPT)

Yesterday, I was meditating on the following verse: "And without faith living within us it would be impossible to please God. For we come to God in faith knowing that He is real and that He rewards the faith of those who give all their passion and strength into seeking Him" (Hebrews 11:6 TPT).

Looking back in my life like at the early days as above, despite how my passion for God varied in my life—sometimes less, sometimes more (sometimes I sought Him less, and sometimes I sought Him more)—my faith was always in Him. I knew He was real, and He always rewarded me. I have gone through some tough times but also great times, but at the end, He has always rewarded me. His presence with me always is His reward. It's His fullness of joy. Every day is a new day! The greatest reward will be when I reach heaven, and I see Him face-to-face. Then I will fall at His feet and tell Him how great He has been, my reward.

Things never discovered or heard of before, things beyond our ability to imagine—

these are the many things God has in store
for all his lovers. (1 Corinthians 2:9 TPT)

Look, It will be a feast; all are welcome to the table!

When Christ shall come with shout of acclamation
And take me home, what joy shall fill my heart!
Then I shall bow with humble adoration
And then proclaim, "My God, how great Thou art!"
Then sings my soul, My Saviour God, to Thee
How great Thou art, how great Thou art
Then sings my soul, My Saviour God, to Thee
How great Thou art, how great Thou art! (Carl Boberg)

12

Heavenly Father Knows What Is Best

They called it a muscle car, V-8 engine, stick shift with a heavy-duty clutch, four-barrel carb, 289ci engine, wide wheel tires, accelerate zero to sixty minutes, like a speeding bullet. The car was a classic 1967 Ford Mustang Fastback 2x2. I got a real good deal on a one-year-old car. I bought it in New York after I decided to move to California. It didn't have too many miles, ready for the long drive. I was proud of it. It drove great all across the country; I enjoyed it. It was God's blessing that I got it from Him.

Except it didn't like San Francisco. There, the roller coaster of its streets didn't suit the heavy-duty clutch, with no power brakes, no power steering, and a stick shift. That was my dream city but not with my car. But once I got out of the town on wide-open roads, it was fun.

Then I got married. God blessed me again with a beautiful wife. My wife hadn't learned how to drive when I met her. Somehow I never got to teach her to drive till she was seven months pregnant. Then, she asked me to teach her. She said it would be more difficult to learn once the baby arrives. I agreed.

After telling her the basics about my car, we went to a parking lot for lessons. I asked her to push the (heavy-duty) clutch with her left leg. She had a hard time and complained she wasn't able to do it. I realized even though I had gotten used to it, it took a lot of strength for her to do that. I told her to use all the might she had. Finally, she did it. Next, I helped her put it into first gear. The car started to move forward. I realized that since the car didn't have power steering or power brakes and had wide wheel tires, it was challenging for her to drive that car, even though I had gotten used to it. So I had to help her turn the steering wheel to the right. It was a very tough car for her to drive, especially seven months pregnant, let alone *learning* to drive.

So after few days, I told her after I came back from work on Monday, we would go to the local Ford dealer and see if we could trade in our car for a four-door with an automatic transmission, power steering, and power brakes so it would be a much more comfortable car for her to drive. I loved that Mustang for the power it had, its design. It was a classic. I checked in Google yesterday; it is still a classic, and a similar car is being marketed at the six-figure price. Now to part with it was hard for me. The many good memories came back. But I felt God would take care of me even if the Mustang was gone.

We went to the dealership on Monday evening. A friendly salesman met us, and we told him what we wanted to see. He showed us several cars, and we liked one of those he showed us. We took a test drive, and both of us liked it. He looked at the difference in the trade-in value for the car we wanted to buy and the one we wanted to trade. It was around $3,000, and we agreed that was fine with us.

Then he said he would take the matter to his manager, took our keys to test drive the Mustang. He returned with an answer that we would need $3,300 for the trade-in and not a penny less. We got upset and walked away. I didn't know God had another reason. My wife was disappointed that she didn't get a car that would have been much easier to drive.

The following day, I went to work, and I got a call from Bill about 11:00 a.m. Bill was a real estate broker we had met with about a week before. He told me that he had just gone to an Open House that morning and had seen a home in a friendly, safe neighborhood. He said that should fit into our finances.

How strange, a new car last night and now it's a house, I thought.

We lived in a one-bedroom apartment then and thought with a baby coming, and it would be nice to buy at least a two-bedroom home if we could afford it. We had met with Bill and worked out what home we could afford and what loan we would pay with what I was making. He asked us how much savings we had, and we had told him about $3,500, so he said he would look for the one that would meet all our requirements.

So when he called me that morning, he said that the house we saw met all the requirements. He asked me if, at my lunch break, he could show us the house. I told him I would check with my wife and call him back. She was okay with it. I called him, told him I would pick her up and meet him at the house at noon. It was a small house with a one-car garage, two small bedrooms, a small room over the garage, but it had a big family room and a nice backyard with fruit trees. We liked the home.

Bill asked, "What do both of you think of this house?"

"Yes, we talked, and both of us like it. But can we afford it?"

He said that he had worked on all the finances and told us that his calculation told him everything would work out with our down payment. As we had talked more, it seemed that we could afford this house. The location was right; it was in West Los Angeles, not too far from my office. We didn't have to work on the house, and it was in the price range we wanted. He said he had already prequalified us for the loan.

He said that the house had come into the market only that morning and said it was priced correctly. He said that we could offer less, but the seller may wait for a few days before he would even consider making you a counter offer. Then, there could be other offers.

"So it'll be your suggestion to offer the full price?" I asked.

"Yes, I think so if you want the house," he answered.

"We would like to make the offer, but I have to get back to my work pretty soon. How about coming to our apartment this evening?"

"Okay, I'll be at your place about 7:00 p.m. In the meantime, I'll tell the listing broker I'll be bringing him an offer this evening."

"Thanks, Bill. See you later."

Bill met us that evening and wrote up the offer, and we signed it. He took it straight to the other broker, who took it to the seller. The next day, we heard from Bill; the seller had accepted our offer.

That evening, I talked to my wife.

"You know what? Something interesting happened."

"What?"

"Two days ago, if we had bought the car, we couldn't have got this house. I think it's God's doing. Sorry to say you have to drive my Mustang, however tough it may be."

"You're right. I'll have to learn to drive. It'll be hard, but the baby will have a room of its own and a big backyard to play in. It'll be our very first home. And it is such a surprise."

The Bible says, "And we know that God causes everything to work together for the good of those who love God and are called according to his purpose for them" (Romans 8:28).

In the case above, how that was true; our Heavenly Father knows what is best for us. *Father knows best!*

"For I know the plans and thoughts that I have for you,' says the Lord, 'plans for peace and well-being and not for disaster, to give you a future and a hope" (Jeremiah 29:11).

When I look back, how wonderful God works all things for good, and even though I thought I was losing my Mustang, we gained our first house. And Priya got her own room.

Marvelous are His thoughts and ways;
how sweet it is!

Every single moment You are thinking of me!

How precious and wonderful to consider that You cherish me constantly in Your every thought!

O God, Your desires toward me are more than the grains of sand on every shore!

When I awake each morning, You're still with me. (Psalm 139:17 and 18)

13

Unexpected Bound to Happen

Times were tough. The economy in the US was slowing down. Jobs as architectural designers in Los Angeles were hard to find. A rose among thorns was a job offer with a well-known architect's firm, Skidmore, Owings, and Merrill, for a one-year contract to work in Iran. Benefits included a flight for the whole family to Iran, paid by the firm on the timeframe suitable to us. This was when the Reza Shah was still the Shah of Iran.

Taking advantage, we made plans for a stopover in Europe for a month. Travel is exciting. Just the thought brought a great feeling. We purchased a three-week Eurail Pass and planned to land in Brussels. My niece, Ramola, lived there with her husband Kelly and their two sons.

The plan was to stay with them when we arrived there, and they would drive us around the countryside in Belgium during the weekends. During the week, we would travel on the train visiting all the great cities. After spending a month in Europe, we would stop in Istanbul on the way to Iran.

All travel arrangements were made. I was greatly looking forward to the trip. My dream of seeing all the architecture I had studied about and seeing them was coming to reality. I bought various lenses for my camera to make sure that I took the best pictures of all the buildings and cities I loved.

Finally, we were on the plane. New places to see, incredible architecture to relish, and dreams were finally coming true. Paris, Rome, Venice—an architectural delight. I was looking forward to it in my mind even as I relaxed on the plane.

After the plane landed in Brussels, we recovered our luggage and proceeded to customs. Once we cleared customs, we were in the immigration line. From standing in the line, we could see all those waiting at the gate for arriving passengers.

There among the crowd, I could see Kelly and Marcus, who is their older son. Their eyes were panning all the incoming passengers, trying to locate us. As soon as I saw them, I waved at them. Their eyes caught me waving, so they waved back.

We had our passports and immigration forms. We gave them to the officer. He looked at them and asked to see our plane tickets. I gave them to him. He stared at all of them, going back and forth. Then he said to me in broken English, "Well, you have marked off that all three of you are staying in Brussels for a month before you leave."

I replied, "Yes, sir."

He answered, "Well, your daughter can stay in Brussels for one month. But both of you will have to take the next plane to Istanbul."

"Take the next plane to Istanbul," his words terrified me—and not me alone, but my wife as well. My mind went crazy. How unusual is his statement? Is he nuts? What is it he's talking about?

"What do you mean, sir? Can you not see all three of us have the same plane tickets? We are all staying here and not leaving for another thirty days. We even bought three-week Eurail passes to travel all through Europe." I replied in a hurry.

He was calm as he answered. "Yes, that's what the ticket says, but you two can't stay in Brussels. You have to take the next flight out of Brussels. Since your next stop is Istanbul, I would suggest that." His voice was firm.

I still couldn't understand him. He just didn't make sense. His statement made me very uncomfortable. After coming so far, how could we not even see Ramola and their family? Now I was perplexed to the point I was getting annoyed. I asked him, "Sir, I don't understand what you are talking about. My niece and family are here in Brussels. Can you explain why you are saying that we can't stay here?"

He replied, "Sir, both of you have Indian passports, and you both need visas to stay in Brussels for a month. But your daughter has a US passport, and she doesn't need a visa to visit Brussels. She can stay here for six months if she wants."

Unexpected indeed; after all, the planning and arrangements we had made, we never checked whether we needed to get visas. It struck me that I hadn't done my homework. His statement being unusual may not be entirely accurate. As bizarre as it may have sounded to me, my assumptions were wrong.

Having lived in the US for so long, we still had only our green cards, hadn't applied for US citizenship, and still had Indian passports. But all our friends had US passports, so they all could travel to Europe without any visas. It never even dawned on me; most of the countries in Europe require visas for Indian citizens. A new challenge on the horizon, I didn't know what to say.

I was dumbfounded. I was in a quandary, "a pickle," I might add. I didn't know what to say. But there was one thing I could do; my prayer was, "Lord, this is my fault. Please let me have the right words to tell him."

"Sir, I have been in the US too long to realize that I needed a visa for Belgium," my words came out in a stammer, "Our daughter was born in the US, and that's how she has the US passport. We have green cards for being in the

US. Our niece and family are here in Brussels. We didn't even think of visas. Is there anything we can do?"

He stared at me for a while. I didn't know whether he was thinking or didn't believe what I was saying. For me, his stare seemed like an eternity. All my dreams of seeing Europe were going up in smoke. It was like he was counting to ten with me being on the floor of a boxing ring after being knocked out. I didn't know if I could get up before he said, "Eight, nine, ten."

I whispered, "Lord, please help us."

Then it was Jesus, who said, "I will never leave you, nor forsake you."

Finally, the Officer spoke, "Why don't you follow me. Let me take you to my supervisor. Let me explain your unusual situation to him."

We followed. I didn't know what to expect. He took us to a room and closed the door behind him. There seemed to be files stacked up on all sides of the room, only a tiny window for the sun to pierce through. Unusual, I thought;

he closed the door behind us? Is this the interrogation process? A man in a uniform starched so crispy that the sleeves could break if one touched them. He seemed very serious. That seriousness was kind of scary.

In the meantime, our daughter seemed to be getting tired and restless. My wife tried to keep her calm. The verse within me was, "I will fear no evil, for You are with me." The officers started talking in their own language. The Immigration officer seemed to be explaining to his superior our situation. After he finished, his superior seemed to ask him a series of questions.

After their conversation was over, the Superior told us in a perfect English voice (took me by surprise), "My officer explained your situation. I'm surprised you never checked your visa requirements. Knowing you had a long flight and your daughter seemed tired, this is what I can do. I'll give you both a forty-eight-hour visa. Once you get into Brussels, you need to make the arrangements if you want to stay longer. I can't tell you what to do, but this will give you a chance to get a thirty-day visa. But I'm warning you if you can't get it, you need to leave Belgium in two days, or you will have dire consequences."

It was a great relief but, at the same time, a warning. I thanked the officer, and he stamped our passports. I mumbled, "Thank You, Lord." My wife breathed a sigh of relief. But my daughter just wanted to get out of that room. She was tired. She was hanging on to her mommy's hand.

Outside, Kelly and Marcus didn't know what was going on behind closed doors. They'd been waiting for hours, it seemed. Those days there were no cell phones and so no communication. He couldn't even call Ramola, who was also kept in suspense.

Finally, we came out to meet them. Unexpected, unusual circumstances; my dreams seemed to die away. For a while, everything seemed to fall apart, but God still had a purpose. It was my mistake; God did keep our dreams alive. Because now I'm His son, he protected me and gave us back our dream. No matter what, God taught me He can turn things around; He is in charge. All I have to do is reach out wherever I am, in whatever circumstances I may have gotten into.

The following two days were grueling. Kelly had to take time off from work. We went to the Belgium Secret Police, Interior Department, and Immigration Department. We stood in long lines, waited for hours in hallways but in the end, and we did get a thirty-day visa to stay—such a relief. Dreams came back alive again. "Thank You, Lord." We did travel for a month as planned and had a wonderful time. God made it all possible.

What a month it was! Kelly took all of us every weekend to a different town and city in Belgium. Then Monday morning, we would get on the train; we had Eurail Pass, which was first class, close to a close-by city like Amsterdam, get off, walk the whole day looking at various spots to sightsee. Then in the evening, we would retake the train and take a long trip to another city, so we get to sleep on the train. We didn't have any reservations or sleeping berths, but this is what we did. First-class compartments had two long seats across facing each other and then a door to close the compartment.

Once we got into the compartment, we would close the door, put our luggage under the seats. Sujita would lie on one seat, and Priya, who was three years old, would lie on the other seat, and I will be sitting next to the window. When people open the door, they will see both sleeping, they will leave. Once the train left the station, we would get that compartment all to ourselves, and I would manage to lie down as well, a little squeezed. The following day, we'll be in another city and do the sightseeing as well.

We did this way of travel, Monday to Friday, and landed at Ramola and Kelly's home Friday evening. Finally, time for showers. What a great experience it was. That way, we traveled for a month. Traveling on the train in Switzerland, we stayed on the train even during the day, since the scenery was so beautiful. So that month went so fast, we had never seen so many beautiful places in so many days. It was so awesome.

The unexpected and the unusual are bound to happen in life. But I found out when I take them to my God, He can always turn things around. Dreams being squashed can come back to life. When I get pressed, I take them to Jesus, and He always comes through! What a difference, He can make in my life! Whether I will or will not take the unusual and unexpected to Him, it's up to me. But when I take them to Him, He always has only good plans for me and a promising future. The same for you too!

"I say this because I know what I am planning for you," says the Lord. "I have good plans for you, not plans to hurt you. I will give you hope and a good future" (Jeremiah 29:11 NCV).

14

Miracle in the Sky

Days of travel had their own intriguing ways. I enjoyed them. New places, different cultures, exciting architecture all made travel a wonderful experience. I had a one-year contract to work as an architect in Iran. This was when the Shah was still in power. At that time, my wife, Sujita, and I had one daughter, Priya, and she was around three years old when we left here.

We traveled for a month in Europe before we landed in Iran. Then we also had a chance to go to India and back a few days in Paris. We had done a lot of traveling; we had some great times of seeing so many places within a year, including Esther's tomb and Persepolis in Iran. I loved the architecture all through Europe on the way going and on the way back. Now it was time to head back home to Los Angeles. At this time, Sujita was seven months pregnant, and Priya was four.

On the way back to Los Angeles from Paris, we had stops in Boston and Philadelphia. We were going to visit friends and relatives in both places. The first stop was good; we met our relatives and saw some fabulous places, including Harvard University. The weather was also good there. It was time to leave for Philadelphia.

We didn't have seat reservations for the flight, and we got to the airport a little late. We got on the plane and found the seats mostly taken. We couldn't find three seats together. So Priya and I found two seats in the middle of the aircraft. Sujita found a seat in the back. We got the last three seats. It was a DC 9, which had about one hundred seats.

The plane took off in time. It was in the evening and getting dark. During the travel days, I never had much time to look at the news or the weather. So I didn't know that there was a storm brewing in Philadelphia. It was instead a short flight. Midflight, the Captain came on the speaker system and announced to everyone to put on their seat belts because there would be a lot of turbulence and jolting.

As the plane got closer to the airport, the weather got more turbulent, and the plane was being tossed more and more. I had a window seat and could see the dark clouds. Suddenly, heavy rain outside and gushing wind took a hefty toll on the plane. There was thunder and lightning as well. I could see the wing go up and down in a frantic way; Priya, sitting by my side, wasn't too frightened and sat quietly since she couldn't see out. She wasn't aware of all the turbulence. But with what I saw outside my window, my heart was pounding.

I knew God was with us and that He was still watching over us. My prayer was like David's prayer, "Please listen, God, and answer my prayer! I feel hopeless, and I cry out to you from a faraway land. Lead me to the mighty rock high above me. You are a strong tower, where I am safe" (Psalm 61:1–3 CEV). I didn't know what was happening in the back of the plane where Sujita was all this time. I didn't have any communication with her because she was too far back.

Then the Captain announced over the intercom that we were approaching Philadelphia airport and getting ready to land. He also warned us to expect more turbulence and keep our seatbelts on. It was still dark outside, with thunder and lightning spanning the skies. Suddenly there was a sudden drop; it felt like a drop of one thousand to two thousand feet. It was like being in a suction cup. I could see the terror in the passengers' eyes. Priya couldn't understand, "What was that, Dad?" All I could say was, "It's just very heavy rain outside," trying to explain it in her terms.

I turned my head and looked outside, and to my amazement, I saw we had fallen off and were just above some three-story buildings. We were so close to the building that the wing of the plane could almost touch it. Our descent was so sudden that we had come down so close to the ground but still traveling at high speed. All I could say again is like what David said,

> *Yea, though I walk through the valley of*
> *the shadow of death,*
> > *I will fear no evil; For You are with me;*
> > *Your rod and Your staff, they comfort*
> *me.* (Psalm 23:4 KJV)

Since the plane was so close to the ground, the Captain tried to apply power to its engines to get it up higher. The plane engines made a loud noise as they tried to raise the aircraft but couldn't get enough thrust to do so. Then the plane started the descent reasonably quickly, with the front of the plane lifted relatively high, and we were sitting on a slope.

Then there was a loud noise even as the plane hit the ground. First, there was a big thud, and then the plane seemed to go on the ground with some heavy bumps on the way. Then it came to a sudden halt. Everything happened so fast. Many overhead storages came down on the passengers; seats had buckled. And when it made a sudden stop, a lot of people hit the front seat. Some people were bleeding; some had fainted. It was chaotic. I tried to look back for Sujita, but I couldn't see her with all the chaos. Priya wanted her mom, but I couldn't help her.

Priya was clinging to me, and I was clinging to the Lord. Sujita was way in the back; I couldn't see her, and Priya couldn't see her mom, even though she desperately wanted her mom.

In the meantime, the stewardess came amid the chaos and opened the door leading to the plane's wing. I picked up Priya and carried her, and I tried to head to the back of the aircraft to locate Sujita with Priya, but the stewardess wouldn't let me go. She kept pushing everyone who stood up to go to the door that she had opened and then to the top of the wing. I had to head toward the wing. There was just no sight of Sujita from where I was. My prayer was "Lord, keep her safe." But even as I left the plane, I looked back; it was a sad scene. So many passengers had either fainted, started bleeding, or were too weak, even to get up.

We had not landed on the runway but on the grass. Now I was on top of the wing carrying Priya. Others were standing over the wing as well. The jump would be about ten feet. It was still raining in a hefty downpour. Some were hesitating to jump. Showing Priya the ground below, I told her to be ready to jump. Holding her tight, we jumped. Even as we fell, the fall was not that bad since there was so much water on the grass from the rain. We made the landing pretty safely so that I was able to stand again holding Priya.

Getting back to looking for Sujita, we were wandering toward the back of the plane. By now, it was totally dark. And still, with a heavy downpour, it was hard to find her. We finally found her. She was wandering around, looking for us, crying hysterically. She kept on calling, "Is my baby all right? Is my baby all right?" Being seven months pregnant, she was distraught that she might have lost the baby. But she was happy to see us.

I looked at the plane. It had come apart in two pieces. The back-end with the restrooms and the kitchen had fallen about one hundred to two hundred feet away. The landing gear had never come out. Landing on the belly in heavily drenched grass, the force had split the plane in two. It was a horrible scene. The back of the aircraft had been torn apart, with a lot of bare metal and wires and a little door to jump ten to twelve feet from the ground. People were standing in the doorway, so high off the ground, frightened to jump from such a great height. And it was still pouring rain in the dark black sky.

Sujita had to jump through all the electrical wires that were tangled up due to the split. Being pregnant, she was so hesitant about the jump, which was about ten to twelve feet, but she didn't have a choice. So after that, she got so worried about the baby.

We hugged each other and looked around for somewhere to get away from the blistering rain. There was nothing around that we could see in the darkness all around us. We were wandering around when a van came by and picked us up. The driver was a plane mechanic who saw the plane hit the ground, headed toward the accident, and picked up people wandering around.

He took us to the hospital that he knew close by. The ride in the van was bumpy, and it took us a while even to get to a road. Sujita was still crying, being worried about the baby. My prayer was for Sujita and the baby, still being thankful to the Lord that He had kept us alive and all together. We ended at the hospital that turned up to be a burn center. The doctors and nurses there were accommodating, checking everyone. After checking Priya and me, they said we were okay and asked us to wait in the waiting room.

After about two hours, they allowed us to visit Sujita. She was still crying when we got there. She said none of the doctors or nurses could find the baby's heartbeat and couldn't determine whether the baby was still alive. There was no obstetrician there, and they had to call for one.

Finally, he came around midnight. He checked her out and told her that the baby was fine. He was able to find the baby's heartbeat, and everything was good. Finally, she stopped crying, and there was a smile. It was rough on all of us. But by the grace of God, we didn't get drowned in anxiety but stayed afloat because of His presence and because of His promises. Jesus promised, "Lo, I am with you always." That was so real in those days.

The following day, this incident was all over the newspapers in Philadelphia. We read the entire story of how the plane was caught in a freak storm and how the plane hit the ground even before the landing gear could come out. They had pictures of the plane, having torn apart, being in two pieces. It also stated that if it were not for the heavy rain, the sparks could have ignited a fire that could have destroyed the plane. And also, it was better to have landed on wet grass without the landing gear. The captain and the copilot were in intensive care, and half the passengers were in the hospital.

Sujita's nerves were much better the next day, but the doctor wanted her to stay at the hospital for another day of observation. The airline had put us in a hotel close by. But we spent the next day mainly at the hospital beside her. We were to take another plane to Los Angeles in three days, about a five-hour plane flight. Priya kept asking us, "Are we getting back into the plane again?" We had to keep her calm. We were kind of nervous about retaking a plane. So we thought of taking the train, which is about a two to three-day journey. But trusting in the Lord, we took the plane. After arriving in LA, we didn't get much news of what happened to the captain and the copilot or the rest of the passengers. But we kept a copy of the Newspaper with pictures of the split plane.

For two months, the baby kept on turning in mom's tummy. About two months later, beautiful Sandhya was born. All I can say is what David had already written, "O taste and see that the Lord is good! Blessed and happy is the man who trusts and takes refuge in Him."

My heart was filled with so much gratitude to God. There was so much excitement when she was born. Excitement filled the air! After so many months of uncertainty, she came hale and healthy. We were jubilant, and we were ecstatic!

Turbulence turned into joy. Miraculous as it was, we had to praise Him; we had to glorify Him. Priya was so happy that she had a little sister. Looking back in my life, the time was short when we had to endure the pain, and very tough, but now after years and years, we can enjoy His goodness in her and for her life. It is hard to praise and thank the Lord when we face perils, but so easy after, but God says to do it even when we go through pain.

> *Most of all, friends, always rejoice in the Lord! I never tire of saying it: Rejoice! Don't be anxious about things; instead, pray. Pray about everything. He longs to hear your requests, so talk to God about your needs and be thankful for what has come.* (Philippians 4:4 and 6 Voice)

Since then, the fundamentals for me always rejoice no matter what, talk to God, always letting Him know of my requests, and be thankful for what has come and also for what is about to come! It was hard, especially when I was in the turbulent plane, then I was only leaning on God, knowing He was with us there.

But faith is being sure of the things we hope for, even if we don't see it as in Hebrews 11. We can expect good things from God even at a turbulent time; even though it is challenging, we can praise Him because all things are possible for Him. He is an incredible God, He can turn the bad circumstance into good, turn things around, and He is always with us even during the turbulent times. After being in a state of agitation, days of uncertainty, and then when the baby is born hale and healthy, there was so much excitement and joy.

There is coming another day full of excitement again! When we live our lives here, especially with COVID, and so much disorder and uncertainty, here we are on earth, maybe one hundred years, but look at the hope we have when we are in heaven for thousands and thousands of years! Isn't that exciting! No more pain, no more bad things, but only fantastic times, incredible times await us. The tremendous excitement I will ever see is when Jesus comes to take me to my heavenly home. That'll be the end of all that I will ever face in this world. Just to see Jesus, it will be worth it all.

It will be worth it all, when we see Jesus!

Life's trials will seem so small, when we see Christ.

One glimpse of His dear face, all sorrow will erase.

So, bravely run the race.

15

Living under the Shadow of the Almighty

This was a few years ago. It was a perfect day—beautiful sunshine, not a cloud in the sky. One day as I was driving to work, the freeways were clear, and I seemed to be getting to the office on time. Just as I was going through a green light at the last intersection before my office, a lady driving her car turned to her left in front of my car without realizing I had the right of way.

It happened all of a sudden; even though I put my foot on the brake pedal with force, her Mercedes just slammed into the front of my SUV. My steering wheel airbag opened, and before I knew it, I was immersed in a vehicle full of smoke, and the burst pillow (airbag) thrust on me, sparks flying with a burning smell as if the airbag was burning. This firework of sparks seemed to go on forever. Then the whole SUV also seemed to stink, with a strange odor penetrating my nose. All of it happened so fast.

When a car crashes, the force required to stop an object is significant because the momentum has changed instantly while the passenger had not. The goal of any supplemental restraint system is to help prevent the passenger while doing as minor damage to them as possible. But that shock of a sudden stop took me surprise and left me stunned for a while.

It took a little time before I realized what had happened and tried to look over the airbag. I saw that both the fronts of the cars were quite bashed in, and the lady driver was slumped over her steering wheel. When I saw the damage to the other vehicle, I wondered whether my SUV did it. Seeing the other driver completely unconscious, my thoughts questioned whether she was even alive.

It was a busy intersection, so many onlookers were pouring in, starring at both the cars. People had come out of the shops and offices since the accident created such a big bang. It was also the corner of the building where my office was located on the fourth floor. I saw people on their cell phones; they could have been calling 911.

I was pinned against the airbag. God had protected me; I didn't even have one scratch. I knew God had saved me and had His arms around me. My mind was at peace, and I was thankful to God that he kept me safe even though both cars were way beyond repair.

I had to push myself out of the airbag. I tried to open my door. But my driver's side door had been jammed. I couldn't open it. I had to reach out to the passenger side door, which did open. I had to push the airbag away, climb over the center console, got into the passenger seat, and then got out. I was able to walk out perfectly normally. I was amazed.

Just then, I heard the noise of a siren and saw an ambulance coming to the scene.

One of my coworkers had heard the noise of the collision and looked down from our office located on the fourth floor of the corner building. He decided to come down to the scene since he saw the state of the cars and saw me in the crowd around them.

Police had come and were redirecting the traffic since one of the streets still had a lot of congestion, and the area was getting clogged. Even as I could get out of the car and walked to the sidewalk, I felt an arm wrap around my shoulder. It was my coworker, who also was an excellent friend of mine. He was stunned it was me that was in one of the cars. He was shocked to see me walking away from my car, whereas the passenger in the other vehicle had utterly lost consciousness. So I realized the crowd was staring at me just walking out of my car completely whole, and others were staring at the other vehicle; the lady slumped over her steering wheel.

"Jey, are you all right? I'm amazed to see you walk away!" that was John from work.

"Me too, I am surprised myself," I replied.

"You look good without a scratch?" he said.

"It all seemed to happen so fast. To be in one piece is God's mercy," I told him.

There was another tap on my shoulder. It was a police officer.

"Sir, were you the one in the car that was involved in the accident?" he asked.

"Yes, Officer."

"Can we go somewhere private so I can ask you few questions?"

"Yes, sir."

He walked me away from that intersection down one of the side streets.

The sound of the high-pitched siren pierced my ears. They were taking the other driver in an ambulance to the hospital.

A verse came to my mind. "You will keep him in perfect peace, whose mind is stayed on You because he trusts in You. Trust in the Lord forever. The Lord is the Rock. The Lord will keep us safe forever" (Isaiah 26:3–4).

Even as the police officer started asking all kinds of questions, I was calm and levelheaded as I answered precisely what happened. Can I be so focused on God that a little thing or major mountains can face me; they wouldn't bother me but keep me calm and relaxed?

Bothering on little or big things can lead us to worry; worry can lead to negative thinking and depression. Why get upset in the first place? Even as I was walking back to my car, which was going to be towed away, I remembered verses from Psalm 91:9–11 (Passion Translation), "When we live our lives within the shadow of God Most High, our secret hiding place, we will always be shielded from harm. How then could evil prevail against us or disease infects us? God sends angels with special orders to protect you wherever you go, defending you from all harm."

The tow truck came and towed my car away. It was a busy day, calling insurance and getting a rental car. Then catching up at work for all the time I lost. I realized that Jesus also promised He would never leave me nor forsake me, and even though everything happened, all of a sudden, He was with me in the midst of all these circumstances.

But throughout it all, I had peace of mind. The image of my walking out of my damaged car unscathed and the idea of the other lady slumped over her steering wheel kept coming back to my mind. I was so thankful to God for protecting me and kept me walk out unscathed. I was praising Him for His incredible protection over me. I was so grateful that I was within the shadow of God Most High, that He sent His Angels to protect me and defend me from all harm!

16

Dreams That Exceed the
Wildest Imagination

Work was going well. The location of my work was next to South Coast Plaza in Costa Mesa was also excellent. Being placed in charge of doing some great projects was also excellent. I also had a great staff to do these projects, getting the projects designed, financed, and built. Our team worked well together—no complaints. We had acquisition managers, architects, development managers, financial analysts, construction managers, and accounting managers, all in a great group of people. We were building about 1,500 apartment units a year, one of the most prosperous areas of our company. We were part of a relatively large company. This company also was a part of a significant savings and loan bank.

Suddenly things snapped. Unbeknown to anyone, one day, a predecessor to FDIC, who oversaw all savings and loans, just raided our bank and took it over. They let all the heads of the bank go. The reasons and the way it happened would be another book to write. There was an announcement that, until further notice, everyone should come to work but not do any work. *That's strange*, I thought. There were lots of rumors floating around. Everyone started to look for other work. Going to work was like going to a morgue, seeing sad and long faces. My prayer was, "Lord, what's happening? Only You know, and I can trust You."

It took a month or so, and finally, there was an announcement. It would be the task of new management to liquidate all properties that the bank owned. There would be an outside real estate group that would be brought in to oversee the liquidation. There would be a select few to work with this group. All the rest would be let go with a severance package.

Being fortunate to be one of the select few, I was offered a post to help the real estate group. My experience had included the full array of the projects, being involved right from acquisition to the end of construction. Being told that if I stayed there until the management was ready to let me go, my severance package would include six-month pay and accumulation of my vacation time until they let me go.

It sounded good to me, and so I stayed until they let me go. Finally, I left there with nine months of pay. That was good and gave me the time to decide my future.

Looking at various options, I decided to go into the development of single-family homes. Taking an option on ten acres of vacant land with a deposit to the owner in a good location in Upland, I started designing the project myself while looking for investors. Finished with the layout and plans, I took them to the city of Upland for eighteen homes.

The process started to go in the right direction, and the city approved the tentative map. Still, I didn't have any investors that could provide equity for the project. Without equity, I couldn't get the construction loan; I couldn't go much further. I met with a coworker named Sita, who used to head up the property management before. I told him about my project and its needs. He told me that he would look for an equity partner.

A few days later, Sita called me. He told me that he found a contractor to build the project and would also provide the equity and the funds to proceed forward. I was able to find a local bank to provide the construction loan based on final approval and permits. Everything came together. I was amazed. I had never done development on my own before, and so I was so thankful to God for how He was solving the jigsaw puzzle for me.

Finally, the permits were issued; all the equity was in, and the construction loan was signed. We posted a large sales sign with a telephone number to call for the buyers interested in buying. We started grading. We were in the process of getting a sales trailer once the grading was complete. In the meantime, I had miniature models made of the homes to be placed in the sales trailer. We had agreed that Sita would be the sales broker. As soon as the sales signs were posted, Sita started receiving calls from potential buyers.

Even though grading had just started and would possibly take another two months, Sita decided to begin his sales pitch. He started making house calls from all those who had called from looking at the sales sign. He placed all the house models in the back of his station wagon, set them up either on the coffee tables or dining tables (in the homes of the ones who called), and made his sales pitch. It is similar to how some sales, including sarees (dress women wear in India), are made in India, doing house calls. We had barely finished the grading, hadn't even started on the slabs, and Sita had already sold all eighteen homes! Sita had become the first door-to-door house salesman that was ever successful to my knowledge. It was incredible. I haven't seen any such sales since either. I was so grateful to God. Now we didn't even need a sales trailer, and that just became our construction trailer. Again, I was amazed.

We were progressed well in the construction of the homes. All the houses had stucco outside, drywall inside, and cabinets were being placed in the kitchen. One day, a Chinese gentleman walked in with a suitcase as I walked through the homes. He showed me a specific house and asked me whether we can go inside that home. I said, "Yes," and I opened up that home. Next thing, he placed the suitcase on top of the center island of the kitchen. Then he opened up the suitcase. It was full of one-hundred-dollar bills. I was awestruck—never seen so much cash. Then, he said that he wanted to purchase that home and if I sold him that house, the suitcase with all that money would be mine. I told him that the home was already sold. He had left that suitcase open, flipped some of the $100 bills, and told me they were real. He asked me what the home was sold for, which my reply was $270,000. He told me that he would offer us $320,000, with all in cash inside, right then and there.

I was bewildered; all the cash right then and there? I called Sita and told him of this offer. He called the buyer and offered to repurchase the home and return their deposit of $5,000. Their answer came back "no" to our offer. Then he called that buyer again and offered $10,000. And the buyer again refused. He said he had already bought all the furniture, and he definitely wanted that house. So we told the Chinese gentleman that we couldn't sell it to him, and he was very disappointed. We later learned that the house was facing a Buddhist temple, which was considered auspicious and special.

Every Tuesday morning, we used to have a partner's meeting at 9:00 a.m. Sita lived in Glendale, Naim, the contractor and partner lived in Beverly Hills, and I lived in Orange County. We all came from different directions, so we may all not get there in time because of the traffic. One Tuesday, Sita and I got there in time, but Naim never got there. So about 9:30 a.m., we called his cell phone but went to his voice mail, so we left a voice mail. We were waiting till 10:00 a.m. and still no Naim, or no return calls either. Then at 10:00 a.m., we called again, his cell phone, and it went to his voicemail. We also had a regular phone in the sales/construction trailer.

A little after 10:00 a.m., the phone in the trailer rang. Sita picked up the phone. It was someone from Naim's house. The housekeeper for Naim called and told us what happened. On the way to the meeting, Naim was stopped by highway patrol at about 8:30 a.m. for speeding. He pulled over to the side and stopped. The officer asked for car registration and his driver's license. He found the registration in the glove compartment. But he forgot where he placed his driver's license.

So Naim called his wife to ask where he may have placed it. She told him that it was in his briefcase and that it was in the car trunk. So Naim said that to the officer, and both went to the back of the car. Naim opened the box and was opening the briefcase. That's when a Domino's car hit both Naim and the officer at full speed. Domino's delivery guy had been working all night long, and he was going home when he fell asleep on the steering wheel. The car lost control when he was sleeping, with his car going full speed and hit both the officer and Naim as they were standing in the back of the vehicle. The freeway had an embankment at the edge of the freeway, and the speed of the Domino's car pushed both Naim and the officer over the embankment, and they both fell about thirty to forty feet. Both were in a critical stage, and they called a hospital helicopter to pick them up. Once they were picked up, they were taken to a local hospital. Then they called his wife, and she told the housekeeper to contact us, and she left to the hospital, to the emergency room.

So the housekeeper called us and told us which hospital they were in, so we rushed to the hospital where he was. We couldn't see him at the hospital, and he was in surgery. We did see his wife, and she was crying. Between the crash from the Domino's car and the thirty to forty feet fall, he had several injuries and many broken bones. After a while, we left. After two days, he died. I felt very sad. I had known him for only six months and but we got along well, and construction of the homes had progressed as envisioned.

There were some sad days. Naim had all the subcontractors; he had all the schedules. He paid all the bills; he coordinated the whole construction. The verse for comfort was this: "He's the hope that holds me and the Stronghold to shelter me, the only God for me, and my great confidence" (Psalm 91:2 Passion). I had to depend on God's strength. I went through all the construction files. I tried to coordinate and start calling the subcontractors. It had been a while I had done construction management.

After two weeks, Naim's wife showed up at the construction scene. She told me she was going to take over the construction. Since Naim was the contractor for the project and he was the one that had invested more than anyone else, Sita and I had to say, "Yes." I turned over all the construction files to her and the construction management. I don't think she had any construction management experience, but I left it all in her hands.

She didn't quite understand the construction sequence, and she was getting upset at some of the subs because she didn't understand their billing. Sita and I can only watch from the outside. We didn't want to get in the middle of what was going on. And we were not happy with what was going on.

I took the matter to God. As David said in Psalm 24 (ERV), "LORD, I put my life in your hands. I trust in you, my God, and I will not be disappointed." Then these verses came back to me. "Give all your worries to Him, because He cares for you" (1 Peter 5:7 ERV). So instructed, I went to the Tuesday meetings and answered the questions when asked, but I never interfered in any construction matters. The project was a little delayed but was getting finished. Sita made sure all the buyer were kept happy. I still attended the meetings when the city inspector or the bank inspector showed up at the site. I tried to be helpful. I was also there when we had a walk-through with the buyers.

Eventually, all things went well. Leaving all things to God, He worked out all things for the good. The buyers were happy; our banker was pleased that all things were well, and as buyers moved in, the construction loan was getting paid off.

One day, I was walking around the homes and watching one of the buyers who was moving into his home. One of the friends of my fathers-in-law stopped by. He asked me how things were, and I told him how all things went well and how all things, including the death of Naim, did not hurt the project but ended up good. He asked me if I had started another project. And I told him I was working on another fifteen homes in Ontario that I was getting plans ready to submit. And he asked me whether I had the financing arranged. I told him I was working on it, but it had not come together. He said he would give the money for the equity that was needed to do that project.

All I can say is God is good. It was a new experience for me. All before, I was always working for someone and was always on the payroll. But here, I had to live by my faith in God. I had to trust Him to arrange all things. He was with me all the way through as promised. And as I saw it, step by step, things were working out, and I had to trust His leading to make my next move.

"Never doubt God's mighty power to work in you and accomplish all this. He will achieve infinitely more than your greatest request, your most unbelievable dream, and exceed your wildest imagination! He will outdo them all, for his miraculous power constantly energizes you" (Ephesians 3:20 Passion).

> What a Friend we have in Jesus,
> All our sins and griefs to bear!
> What a privilege to carry
> Everything to God in prayer!
> O what peace we often forfeit,
> O what needless pain we bear,
> All because we do not carry
> Everything to God in prayer!
> (Joseph M. Scriven)

17

Living in the Blessings

I had built ten homes in Woodland Hills, CA. They were big, between 3000 to 4000 SF each, and the lots were all half acre each. They were all well done and were beautiful. But the times were getting tough. California's job market was drying up, and buyers were few. I did have a broker to sell the homes, but he said he'll have open houses only during the weekends. So during the week, if I had free time, I would do open houses. Most of the time, I would be there by myself—not many visitors.

One day, I was doing an open house, and I saw three big men heading toward where I was doing the Open Homes. All three were tall, well-built, and big. They were all in a suit and good-looking. I wondered who they were. The door opened, and all three came in. The first introduced himself to me. He said, "My name is Jean-Claude

Van Damme, and I would like to see your houses." I imme-diately recognized him. I had seen him in some movie trailers and a couple of his movies out of his sixty films. I replied, "Yes, sir. We have three models. Would you like to see all the three models?" He replied, "Yes, please."

So we headed out to the first model. The sun was bright, and it was getting hot. He started taking his tie and gave it to one of his bodyguards. Then he started taking his jacket and gave it to the other guy. Then he started taking off his shirt and gave it to the first. Within two minutes, he was showing off his well-built muscle chest.

We had a good talk along the way. I started talking about his movies. He started telling me about all the ones he was involved in. Then I took him to the models, and he was asking me a lot of questions. The other two guys with him were very quiet; they hardly said a word. He said he wanted to see what he was buying for his ex-wife. Then he told me that he would bring her and see what she liked if he liked them. He was amiable; I got to know him well and showed him all the three models.

After seeing all the three models, he asked me what time I closed up the open house. I told him about 4:00

p.m. Then he pulled up one of his business cards, gave it to me, said, this is where I live, and asked me to come to his house and have dinner with him. I was surprised to get an invitation for dinner at his home.

So after I closed up the complex, he left for Jean Claude's home, and I was surprised it was not too far from my homes. He had a beautiful home. I rang the doorbell, and someone opened the door. He asked me who I was looking for. I said, "Jean-Claude Van Damme." He went in, and Jean Claude came out and said, "Jey, glad you made it. Come on in." He introduced me to everyone that was there. His wife was there, his kids were there, and his mother-in-law was there. They were all charming and joking around, which made me very welcome.

Jean Claude gave me a tour of his home and took me to his big backyard. Then he opened the door to something that looked like another big house. There was a big gym. It was huge, like another fitness place with all sorts of equipment, weight machines, and some machines I had never even seen before. It was quite a gym.

Then I went and had dinner with his whole family. That day was a day of remembrance for me. I never had a movie star treat me like that before. One day, I was a stranger and the next day looks like I had a best of friends. This reminded me of a story I read in the Bible.

One hot summer afternoon, Abraham was sitting by the entrance to his tent near the sacred trees of Mamre when the Lord appeared to him. Abraham looked up and saw three men standing nearby. He quickly ran to meet them, bowed with his face to the ground, and said, "Please come to my home where I can serve you. I'll have some water brought so that you can wash your feet, then you can rest under the tree. Let me get you some food to give you strength before you leave. I would be honored to serve you."

"Thank you very much," they answered. "We accept your offer."

Abraham quickly went to his tent and said to Sarah, "Hurry! Get a large sack of flour and make some bread." After saying this, he rushed off to his herd of cattle and picked out one of the best calves, which his servant quickly prepared. He then served his guests some yogurt and milk together with the meat.

While they were eating, he stood near them under the trees, and they asked, "Where is your wife, Sarah?"

"She is right there in the tent," Abraham answered.

One of the guests was the Lord, and he said, "I'll come back about this time next year, and when I do, Sarah will already have a son." (Genesis 18:1 to 10 CEV)

This happened when Abraham was one hundred years old and Sarah was ninety years old. Suddenly, they received a baby when they were that old, as God's blessing. A newborn baby when he was one hundred. God's blessing can happen at any time. It could be a suddenly. It was an unexpected blessing that I found a great friend who the day before was a stranger. It was a suddenly. Abraham was called a friend of God, sitting by his tent door in the heat of the day, which was like any other day. And suddenly, a promise of a newborn.

The promise of a baby and then the baby was born!

Proverbs 10:22 (CEV) says, "When the LORD blesses you with riches, you have nothing to regret."

I found out knowing Christ; I can live in the blessing of God, in every area of my life, relationally, in my spirit, body, and soul, physically, financially, and in all my dealings and all my circumstances. There is God's Word. Then there is the promise for me in there, even as I meditate in it, and the promise becomes a blessing! And I have nothing to regret. Watch another verse from Galatians 3:14 (Voice): "This is what God had in mind all along: the blessing He gave to Abraham might extend to all nations through the Anointed One, Jesus; and we are the beneficiaries of this promise of the Spirit that comes *only* through faith."

God's Word tells me I am a beneficiary of His promise and receive even the blessing of Abraham because I know Christ, His promise of His Spirit through faith. His presence with me always is a blessing. And His promises become blessings! It could be a suddenly. That's wonderful news for me!

18

Miracles Still Happen

Toward the end of 2005, we were invited to my nephew's son's wedding in India that was to happen in January of 2006. I decided to go since I get to meet my sisters and all my relatives at the wedding, some I have not seen for a long time. It is a very gala affair; I enjoy the food, the festivities, and the music. My wife or none of our kids couldn't go in the middle of their school days, but I decided to go by myself. Usually, on the way to Madras, I like to stop somewhere and sightsee. This time, I decided to stop in Bombay, where my cousin lives. I wrote to her, and she asked me to stay with them. I left after Christmas and stopped at Bombay for four days.

Her husband had arranged for his driver to pick me up at the airport, and I arrived at her house in a lovely part of Bombay. He was head of a bank, and so I had an excellent time visiting with them. I did do a lot of walking and sight-seeing and taking many pictures. I did eat most of the time at home. She had many chicken livers, hearts, and other parts, which in India at that time were called delicacies. The last day I was there, my right foot started hurting and started swelling up.

I took the flight on the fourth evening to Madras, and my nephew was there at the airport to pick me up. When I arrived there, my foot was still swollen and painful. I also had a hard time walking. His brother-in-law was an ortho-pedic surgeon, and he arranged for him to see me the fol-lowing day. After he saw my foot, he sent me to a Lab to get my blood tested. He found out from the lab that I had a high urea level and told me that I had gout.

He prescribed Allopurinol, and he said I might have to take it for life. He asked me several questions and found out I was eating chicken livers and delicacies, and he told me they contain high levels of proteins and that must have triggered gout, that I should no longer eat them. He also said if I have pain, I can take pain pills. I started taking those pills. He also suggested avoiding walking but also be seated with my right foot lifted on the table. I did all he had told me, but my swelling didn't go down. I stayed with my sister, and I had my leg lifted on her coffee table and spent most of the time talking to her. I had gone there to meet all my relatives for the wedding but stayed most of the time indoors because of my foot.

Few days before the wedding, there was a dinner for all the relatives and friends of the bridegroom. It was a formal affair, and I was invited. I had to wear and a suit and tie. But my leg was still swollen, and so I can put on only flip-flops. A suit and a tie with flip flops weren't a great sight to appear, especially at a wedding. Everyone that knew me came to greet me and saw my flip-flops, and had questions for me. I had to explain what happened to everyone. I asked the Lord to help me to heal my foot, but there was no answer.

Two days later, there was the engagement dinner. This was in a big hall with a big stage about three feet high with steps leading to it. I was sitting in the audience, and then I heard my name being called out for me to go up to the stage and pray with the microphone for the occasion. My foot was still swollen, and I was still wearing flip-flops. There I was, walking up the open stairs on flip-flops and a suit. I was so embarrassed. For those who didn't know me, to watch me walking to the stage with the suit and flip flops must have thought this guy was a lunatic.

My foot was still swollen on the wedding date, and I was mixing in the crowd; not many could see my flip-flops, but I was so glad. Nobody stepped on my foot, especially on the swollen foot. And if they did, I would have been screaming amid the crowd.

So my trip was finally over, and the swelling finally subsided a little. And in the long flight home, I was able to rest my foot, since the next day, I had to go back to work, and I had to wear my shoes. But it was so painful since there was still some swelling. After I came back to the US, I made an appointment to see my doctor. She saw my foot and had me get a blood test. I did, and the urea level had come down a little bit but still high. She also recommended the tablet Allopurinol every day and pain pills every time I needed it. So I followed her advice, and slowly all my swelling went down and was back to normal. Then suddenly, I would get an attack, and then I would take my pain pills. This was a routine occurrence.

After a few years, I was listening to someone called Andrew Wommack. He was teaching on Mark 11:22 to 24:

> *So Jesus answered and said to them,*
> *"Have faith in God. For assuredly, I say*
> *to you, whoever says to this mountain, 'Be*

removed and be cast into the sea,' and does not doubt in his heart, but believes that those things he says will be done, he will have whatever he says. Therefore, I say to you, whatever things you ask when you pray, believe that you receive them, and you will have them.

He said, any problems that I have or that I face, I can say to the problem (like a mountain), "Be removed and be cast into the sea," and "in Jesus's name." And he also added that I should not have any doubt in my heart and believe that those things I had said, will be done, as Jesus said.

He said it could be a sickness or a problem facing me, could be a huge problem that is blocking me, I can say to it, be cast into the sea in Jesus's Name. But after I say that, I should not doubt that it isn't going to happen but fully believe that it is going to happen; that the Name of Jesus is so powerful that God has put everything under Jesus's control according to 2 Corinthians 15:27. I started meditating on the Bible verses and his message. I started thinking if gout was my big problem, can I not say to it, being my mountain, can I not command it to be cast into the sea, in Jesus's name? Can I not have a "bulldog faith" in my Lord, that He can heal me? Like a bulldog, once I bite into the faith, it's never letting go. Faith is never giving up.

He already paid the price for my healing. I read the passage Isaiah 53:5, "But Jesus was wounded for our transgressions, He was bruised for our iniquities; the chastisement for our peace was upon Him, And by His stripes, we are healed." He bore the stripes by the Roman soldiers on His back and the wounds He also bore on the cross; that was the price for my healing. So all I have to do is believe what He already paid this price for me, ask His forgiveness, and to say to my problem or sickness to be removed from me, to believe the sickness is gone and not doubt His words. Then upon accepting, I need to thank Him for His promises with praise and worship to Him, for what He did, and for His promise, it will happen.

For about a few days, my foot was normal. Suddenly, it started hurting again. I began to hobble. The pain was excruciating. I was going for my pain pills. My memory went back to the passage in Mark, and I started meditating on that. Can I say what Jesus said about having faith in God and say to gout, "gout be cast into the sea in Jesus's name"?

Yes, I said that. I also thanked Him for His promises because I believed it would happen. But nothing happened.

I waited, but it was hurting quite a bit, so I took a pain pill and sat down for a while. Did I not have faith? Did I have to take the pain pill? Eventually, I was able to walk normally, and the pain went away.

Then, I was reading another passage. "Keep on asking, and you will receive what you ask for. Keep on seeking, and you will find. Keep on knocking, and the door will be opened to you" (Matthew 7:7 NLT). So that means, one try and instantly if I thought it didn't work, would I give up? So I decided that every time gout acts up, and I get in pain, I will say, "Gout, in the Name of Jesus, be gone and be cast into the sea." Then I thanked and praised God for His sacrifice for me. After a couple of times, I found out that I just said it and believed that would go away, and I didn't take the pain pill. It waited three to four hours, had to bear the pain, but believed in the Lord, and the pain went away.

So every time the gout attack came, I said, "Gout in Jesus's name, leave" and thanked the Lord, then the pain would leave in two or three hours, and after a few days, in one hour and one instant, the pain left right away. The more I did, and the pain went away, the stronger my faith became. Then it could be five minutes or maybe twenty minutes. I just had to stand firm. I started praising Him because His promises came true. After a while, I stopped taking pain pills altogether. Then eventually, I stopped even taking Allopurinol, and still the same result. Then I made a doctor's appointment, and I saw the doctor. I told him my gout does not bother me anymore, and I had stopped taking Allopurinol and the pain pills. He said he was okay with that. And he said, if gout starts bothering me again, I can begin to retake them.

I stopped taking pills altogether. It did come back and attack me sometimes. But I would just say what Jesus asked me to say, and every time it went, sometimes five minutes and sometimes twenty minutes, and the pain would leave, and I was able to walk normally. Then it became a rarity, and then, the swelling never came back. I was praising God. It was a matter of having complete faith in Christ that I asked for and that I should not have any doubts, unbelief, and wavering on my faith. No more running for pain medicine, but I commanded gout to leave wherever I was, and the pain left me. Miracles still happen!

I was reading a story on Luke 17:12–16, "And as they entered a village there, ten lepers stood at a distance, crying out, "Jesus, sir, have mercy on us!" He looked at them and said, "Go to the Jewish priest and show him that you are healed!" And as they were going, their leprosy disappeared. One of them came back to Jesus, shouting, "Glory to God, I'm healed!" He fell flat on the ground in front of Jesus, face downward in the dust, thanking him for what he had done."

All Jesus did was to tell the lepers to show the Jewish priest (who was like a doctor at that time) that they were healed. At the time Jesus spoke to them, they were not healed because it says, as they were going, their leprosy disappeared. So they left Jesus and went by faith, and as they were going, their leprosy left, and they were healed. Only one returned, shouting, "Glory to God, I'm healed." So faith is the key as well as shouting praises. The best part is now I don't even get the attacks of gout anymore. I also shout, "Glory to God, I'm healed." It was so true in my life. My heart is so full of gratitude for what Jesus did for me on the cross.

> *Jesus healed all those who were sick.*
> *So He made clear the full meaning of what*
> *Isaiah the prophet said:*
> *"He took away our diseases*
> *and carried away our sicknesses."* (Matthew
> 8:16p–17 Passion)

Yes, Jesus healed me, totally set me free from my disease. He took it away. He carried it away. Healing is a part of my salvation in Jesus, just as much as the forgiveness is for my sins. He healed everyone that asked Him for healing. Now, I can sing the old hymn, as below!

He healeth me, oh, bless His name!
I want to spread abroad His fame;
From dread disease, He sets me free,
The Lord, my healer, strong is He!
He healeth me, He healeth me!
By power divine He healeth me;
He healed the sick in Galilee,
And now by faith, He healeth me!

(Manie Ferguson)

19

On Earth, as It Is in Heaven

On the way back on one of my office trips, I saw a friend at the Los Angeles Airport, heading for the Departure Terminal. I had known Randy and his wife, Rose, for several years.

So when I saw him, I greeted him, "Hi, Randy, it's so nice to see you. How are you?"

He said, "Hey, Jey, I'm doing fine. Where are you returning from?"

"From Phoenix. I've been going there several times, finding sites for new projects. So where are you going this time?"

He replied, "I'm headed to Bangkok, Thailand."

"Wow! Quite far away! How long are you going for?"

"I'm going to be there for three years at least, maybe more, depending on how things go."

I said, "Three years, that's a long time. Bangkok—must be an interesting place. I'm thinking of going to India next year. Do you mind if I stop in Bangkok on the way and you can show me around? I usually stop at a different city on the way to India, stay for a few days, and sightseeing. It would be cool to see Bangkok."

"Definitely, let me know when you are coming, and you can stay with us. I'll have someone pick you up. Here's my card. Send me an email when you are coming. Bye."

So we parted company. I looked at his business card. I just found out that he was the president of Union Oil for Southeast Asia. My thinking just went haywire. All along, I knew him as just a guy working at Union Oil, and he had been there a long time. My thoughts, *Wow! What a position! To be in a big oil company and then to be in charge of the whole of South-East Asia; all these years I had known him, he was such a humble guy.*

The following year, there was a wedding in India just after Christmas. When I attend a wedding in India, I get to see all my relatives in one place without visiting each one at a time. And also enjoy Indian weddings—lots of great memories. So I decided to go to the wedding. My wife didn't want to go, so I asked my son whether he wanted to go with me. Since it was his winter break, he decided to join me. I decided to email Randy whether my son and I can stop in Bangkok for a few days to sightsee.

He replied to my email, "That would be fine," and he told me that he and his wife would be in town and for us to spend as many days in their home as we liked. He also asked me to send the flight information, and he would have his driver pick us up. We decided to stop for four days on the way. I made the flight arrangements, and I sent an email to Randy with the necessary details. I just prayed, *Lord, did I do the right thing? I seem to tread in unknown waters; if it's Your will, please let it all go smooth!*

That Saturday, we had an international student get-to-gether that I volunteer. I had picked up some students on the way. I met a Korean student I had known for some time. After our pleasantries, I told him I was going to India for a wedding, and on the way back, I had a one-day stopover in

Seoul, Korea. He asked me what that day was going to be like. I told him that it was going to be a Saturday. Then he asked me if he could arrange for his friend in Seoul to give me a tour of Seoul on that day. I said that would be great. He asked me to provide him with all the details, and he will send it to his friend at the airport to pick me up. Again my thoughts, *Was this again God who sent Kim, just like meeting Randy?*

The day arrived, and we left for Bangkok. As promised, Randy's driver was at the other end waiting for us with a placard. He drove us to Randy's home. Having never been to Bangkok, I found it to be an exciting city. Buddhist monks in saffron robes seemed to be everywhere. Golden temples with their domes and steeples seem to sprinkle the city. It was modern and ancient, all combined. Traffic was as crazy as it was in Madras.

The driver drove us out of the city to beautiful suburbia intermingled with native homes built on sticks over waterways. Then we entered a driveway behind private gates. The driveway led into a beautifully manicured landscaped garden to a fifteen-story building. He took us through a fabulous lobby to the elevator, which took us to the penthouse. The driver told us that Randy had the whole penthouse.

Randy and his wife Rose met us at the elevator. After our greetings, they showed us around. All the floors were granite. The furniture was all made of teak inlaid with marble. The countertops were all made of marble. There were many windows and balconies with such incredible views. When I looked down, there was a large river wrapping around three sides of this building. Many exciting boats were crisscrossing the river. I could have stayed there forever, watching everything happening below.

Then he took us to our room. Again, everything was granite, teak, and marble. Beautiful headboards capping the bed, the desk, and the dressers were unique, all in teak wood. They were fascinating. We walked into our bathroom, and again it was a great surprise. Even the whole bathtub was made of marble; it seemed to have been carved out. It even had Jacuzzi jets. It looked like everything there was a piece of art. We went out to the balcony, and again, we were amazed by the views.

Randy came and invited us for dinner. We were seated around a beautifully decorated dining table and were treated to a six-course dinner. I had a question for Randy at the table. Some of the windows are wide open, and there are no screens in any of them; what about the mosquitoes?

He replied, saying they don't get above the eighth floor, so being on the fifteenth floor, there's no fear of any of them getting in. Something I learned that day.

Rose told us that she would show us Bangkok the next day. She had the whole day all planned for us. That night, when I went to bed, I thanked the Lord, with joy for such a great day, for giving such great friends like Randy and Rose. I was so grateful to God.

After having breakfast at home, the next day, we visited the King's Palace and some of the temples around. There were so many golden-clad domes and steeples we had never seen. Everything was so grand; we enjoyed our morning so much. Then Rose took us to a great Thai restaurant for lunch and did more sightseeing in the afternoon. Again, that night, I was praising God for the great day He gave us.

The next day, Randy had arranged for his driver to take us around. We had another wonderful full day, and days that are more wonderful lay ahead of us. The four days went so fast. Those days were incredible. They were memorable. Even my son was amazed. Years have gone by, but that trip sticks in my mind. I couldn't have asked for a better place and a better time. After being there in awe for four days, it was like being in heaven on earth. I was thanking my God for such beautiful days He gave us.

We thanked Randy and Rose and left for India, and time went there very fast. The wedding was great; we met so many wonderful relatives and friends. We had excellent Indian food that I love and enjoyed myself; I met all my relatives. Even Suresh enjoyed the trip well. Now it was time to head back. But this time through Seoul, Korea.

We left Madras, India, and arrived in Seoul at 6:00 a.m. the next day, a Saturday. By the time we left the plane and checked out, we were outside about 6:30 a.m. We saw a big sign in the waiting crowd, "Samuel," and we knew that was meant for us. So I waved back and greeted the two waiting for us. A friend of my friend in the US was there and had bought another friend of his. We greeted each other, and they spoke broken English, but we managed to get along. We got into their car, and we drove into the city.

This was in January, so it was cold in Korea, and there was still snow on the ground. We had gone to India, where it was warm, and we were still in our shirts. All we had was a suit jacket we had taken for the wedding. But in twenty-degree weather, it hardly kept us warm, and we were freezing.

Our hosts took us to a top of a hill where you can see quite a bit of Seoul from the top. Because at 7:00 a.m., nothing was open, so they thought we would enjoy seeing Seoul from the top. As we were getting out of the car, we were shivering. It was a fantastic view to see.

They took us to the King's Palace, but we had to wait to get in since we got there too early. Then we went to a Buddhist temple. His friend had to leave and said bye to us. After that, he took us for lunch at a traditional Korean restaurant. We took off our shoes, took a small mat to sit on, and the three of us sat around a circle on a wooden floor. Then they bought a huge table full of different dishes in small bowls and placed it in the middle. There must have been about sixty dishes. Our hosts said, "Please eat," but they would not tell us what everything was. So after we finished eating, they told us what we ate. You'll not want to know what we ate.

Then we went to a Korean teahouse, a shopping street, a market, a park, all in one day. Our plane to the US was going to take off at 10:30 p.m., and so our day was filled with so many great things to see. Everything was new to our eyes and curiosity to the soul. So finally, when we got to sit back in our plane seats, we realized how amazing the whole trip had been and how good our God was, in so many unique ways.

I was thinking of all the great things that one trip was, especially the penthouse of Randy and Rose, that incredible place of marble, granite, and teak; it reminded me of a passage that Jesus told us in John chapter 14. This is what He said, "In My Father's house are many mansions; if it were not so, I would have told you. I go to prepare a place for you. And if I go and prepare a place for you, I will come again and receive you to Myself; that where I am, there you may also be." Suddenly, it dawned on my mind, one day, I am going to living in my mansion in heaven, maybe even glorious than Randy's, with Jesus. He promised He is preparing a mansion for me, and He is coming back to get me to go there with Him and live in a mansion. I believe it and am dreaming of that date.

I know I can droll over the place that Rand has now, but no longer. When I live in my mansion in heaven, no more, my faith is in the Words of Jesus; what a day that will be.

> I'm satisfied with just a cottage below
> A little silver and a little gold
> But in that city where the ransomed will
> shine
> I want a gold one that's silver-lined

I've got a mansion just over the hilltop

In that bright land where we'll never grow
old

And someday yonder we will never more
wander

But walk on streets that are purest gold

Don't think me poor or deserted or lonely

I'm not discouraged I'm Heaven bound

I'm but a pilgrim in search of a city

I want a mansion, a harp, and a crown

I've got a mansion just over the hilltop

In that bright land where we'll never grow
old

And someday yonder we will never more
wander

But walk on streets that are purest gold.

(Ira Stamphill)

20

What a Glorious Morning

On a Saturday, early in 2014, I was reading my Bible after I got my coffee. I didn't have anything planned for that day. So I kept reading and pondering over various verses. I seemed to be enjoying reading the Bible and kept reading. Meditating was a time I enjoyed because that is the time God was talking to me. Time didn't matter, and I realized I had spent over three hours. And I had enjoyed it.

Before that day, I had spent only twenty to thirty minutes a day reading and meditating on my Bible. That day was a turning point in my life. That Saturday day, I decided that I will spend at least one hour every day. And amazingly enough, the time I spend with my Bible has been so good, and it is as if the Holy Spirit speaks to me every day.

Over time, I bought an interacting Bible for my laptop and also started using my iPad. I use various translations, I copy and paste verses, I write prayers using multiple verses. My spiritual life has been changing for the better.

In April 2014, early morning, just before I woke up, but my eyes were still closed, I saw in front of me at a distance, bright shining white light or a white brightness so bright to see. This went on for a while. Even as I gazed upon that brightness, I saw strobes of white lights start flashing across in front of me. This also went on for quite a while. I was in awe the whole time. Then I hear myself screaming to shout at the top of my voice, "I love You, Jesus!"

That shout woke me up stunned and dazed, and I sat upon my bed just going over and over what I saw and heard of my shouting. I went on to read my Bible, but my mind was a bit unsettled on what I read the whole time. I couldn't concentrate on reading my Bible. Then the day got busy, but at times that scene would burst back into my mind.

In a couple of days, in my quiet time, meditating with the Bible, I came across Matthew 17 (The Passion Translation):

> Six days later, Jesus took Peter and the two brothers, Jacob and John, and hiked up a high mountain to be alone.
>
> Then Jesus' appearance was dramatically altered. A radiant light as bright as the sun poured from his face. And his clothing became luminescent—dazzling like lightning. He was transfigured before their very eyes.

Another translation, Matthew 17:2 "While these followers watched him, Jesus was changed. His face became bright like the sun, and his clothes became white as light."

That was what I saw, Jesus's face became bright like the sun and a radiant light as the sun poured out from His face, and His clothes became luminescent—dazzling light lightning, and as white as light. And it was so bright that I could not see Jesus nor His face; it was too bright for my eyes, but my spirit saw the face of Jesus, and that is why my spirit shouted out, "I love You, Jesus."

Whether it was a dream or a vision, and in reality, what it will be like when I get to see Him face to face. It was glistening and sparkling white so as no man living can stare into His glory and live. It was too much for the natural Eye. But for my spirit, who is in the Holy Spirit, saw Jesus in all His beauty and shouted out, "I love You, Jesus."

The strobes of white light were as described in Habakkuk 3:4, "Rays flashed from His hand, and there He veiled His power."

Those rays of light were amazing. It could have been like lightning but was straight lines rather than in a crooked fashion as in lightning, but so much energy came in such power.

It was glorious, wonderful, and incredible. It reminded me of the verse, "But as it is written: Eye has not seen, nor ear heard, Nor have entered into the heart of man; The things which God has prepared for those who love Him" (1 Corinthians 2:9 (NKJV).

His Majesty could not be seen, nor was any image, because of His splendor too extreme to bear.

Again a song tells it all:

> The splendor of the King,
> clothed in Majesty;
> let all the earth rejoice, all the earth rejoice.
> He wraps himself in light
> and darkness tries to hide,
> and trembles at his voice, and trembles at
> his voice.
> How great is our God,
> sing with me: how great is our God.
> And all will see how great, how great is
> our God.
> And age to age He stands,
> and time is in His hands;
> beginning and the end, beginning and the
> end.
> The Godhead, Three in One,
> Father, Spirit, Son,
> the Lion and the Lamb, the Lion and the
> Lamb,
> How great is our God… Name above all
> names,
> Worthy of all praise;
> my heart will sing: how great is our God.

How great is our God... (Chris Tomlin)

So many times since then, that vision keeps coming back to me so alive; it was just like it happened yesterday. That shout of mine, "I love You, Jesus," keeps resounding in me so many times. It has been so special to me. I treasure this experience as an extraordinary occasion for me.

What a glorious morning it was; how great is our God!

21

The Love of the Father

It was a few days after I saw in the glorious brightness, my spirit saw Jesus and said, "I love You, Jesus." Early on another morning, I was reading my Bible, and I had my eyes closed as I was meditating on a verse when I saw myself walking very slowly. It looked like I wasn't feeling good. I didn't look happy. I seemed depressed and rejected. I saw myself wearing worn-out, torn, dirty clothes, seem to be all tattered, with a bad smell so strong.

I saw in the distance someone running toward me. He got closer and closer; He seemed to be an older person. He came running toward me, hugged me, grabbed me in my waist, twirled me around and around, started kissing me on my cheeks over and over again.

That was all. I opened my eyes. There I was again puzzled, another dream or a vision? What I saw seemed so natural, so real. He was running toward me, He grabbed me,
He was twirling me, and He was kissing me on my cheek,
and everything seemed so real. I kept going back to what I
saw. Everything happened so fast, just like in less than five
minutes. Even after seven years, it seemed like it happened
yesterday.

I was still thinking about what I saw and felt, how
depressed I looked. The way I was walking and feeling
when I saw myself, in the beginning, was like the story of
the prodigal son. Yes, like the prodigal son.

I went back to read the Bible passage of the prodigal
son, and below is what I read.

> *Then Jesus said, "Once there was a
> father with two sons. The younger son came
> to his Father and said,*
>
> *"'Father, don't you think it's time to give
> me the share of your estate that belongs to
> me?'*
>
> *"So the Father went ahead and distrib-
> uted among the two sons their inheritance.*

Shortly afterward, the younger son packed up all his belongings and traveled off to see the world. He journeyed to a far-off land where he soon wasted all he was given in a binge of extravagant and reckless living.

"With everything spent and nothing left, he grew hungry, for there was a severe famine in that land. So he begged a farmer in that country to hire him. The farmer hired him and sent him out to feed the pigs. The son was so famished, and he was willing even to eat the slop given to the pigs because no one would feed him a thing.

"Humiliated, the son finally realized what he was doing, and he thought, 'There are many workers at my Father's house who have all the food they want with plenty to spare. They lack nothing. Why am I here dying of hunger, feeding these pigs and eating their slop? I want to go back home to my Father's house, and I'll say to him,

"'Father, I was wrong. I have sinned against you. I'll never be worthy to be called your son. Please, Father, just treat me like one of your employees.'

"So the young son set off for home. From a long distance away, his Father saw his son coming, dressed as a beggar, and great compassion swelled up in his heart for his son who was returning home. So the Father raced out to meet him. He swept him up in his arms, hugged him dearly, and kissed him over and over with tender love." (Luke 15:11–20 The Passion Translation)

Yes, I was like the young man who was so starved, humiliated, and dressed as a beggar in what I remembered. And the Father that was racing to meet me was the Heavenly Father. His love for me was so strong, even though I was so dirty, filthy, tattered clothing, an awful stench so strong, yet He hugged me, kissed me over and over with tender love. I realized He loves me so much. No matter how I felt, his passion for me was so strong; it overtook my whole being. What does the Bible say?

Look with wonder at the depth of the Father's marvelous love that he has lavished on us! He has called us and made us his very own beloved children. The reason the world

*doesn't recognize who we are is that they
didn't recognize Him.* (1 John 3:1 Passion)

All I could remember was, He swept me up, grabbed me, hugged me, twirled me, and kept kissing me with His tender love.

Again, this too, this vision keeps coming back to me so strong, over and over again, like yesterday. I can never forget. How can I? He loves me so, so, so much. How can I ever forget? He that ran toward me is the same God who created the galaxies, the earth, the sun, the moon, the stars, the Universe, all the people, and the animals. His love for me is so incredible; He filled me so much in love. I am His new creation.

Second Corinthians 5:17 (NKJV) tells me, "Therefore, if anyone is in Christ, he is a new creation; old things have passed away; behold, all things have become new."

That's a great mystery, the One that created the galaxies. Wow! He hugged me, and I dwell in Him and He in me. It takes faith.

Ephesians 3:17 says, "That Christ may dwell in your hearts by faith."

Now I am no longer famished and depressed, but now I walk contented and satisfied. I am blessed; I am highly favored—what a God I have. It all started because I spent three hours reading and meditating on the Bible about eight years ago on a Saturday. Incredible as it was, then on, I began spending at least an hour a day in God's Word, even on a busy day. I got hungry for His Word, then all the blessings that came after, intimacy started after, I can only thank and praise Him.

Another verse I saw.

Jesus: "If you, imperfect as you are, know how to lovingly take care of your children and give them what's best, how much more ready is your Heavenly Father to give a wonderful gift to those who ask Him?" (Matthew 7:11 Passion).

Jesus said the Father is ready to give beautiful gifts to those who ask Him. As His child, I can ask and receive beautiful gifts. Since then, God's favor started; so many dreams on and off—sometimes in surprises, some at night, some in my daydreams. Could that be the same for you? Is COVID worrying you? And what else? Just spend an hour every day in the Bible; it is worth the sacrifice. Worship

Him in spirit and truth, be intimate with Him, and just watch and see the blessings and favor of the Lord to follow You!

> Love so mighty and so true
> It merits my soul's best songs
> Faithful, loving service, too
> To Him belongs.
> Love lifted me (2)
> When nothing else could help
> Love lifted me.

22

The Third and Fourth Dreams

A few days later, I had gone to bed to sleep; as usual, I turned all the lights off. It must have been about 11:00 p.m. I went to sleep. I was asleep when I saw a bright white light facing right at me. It seemed to have dark brown rings around it. That light seemed to keep stirring at me for a long time. Suddenly my eyes opened, and the room was so dark. Then I looked at the clock, and it was twelve thirty. I sat up in darkness. That bright light was vivid, and I just had seen it being so brilliant. I was wide awake now, thinking about what I had seen. After a while, I went back to sleep. The following day, I woke up, and what I had seen came back to my mind. During the day, I would think back on what I had seen.

The next night, I went to sleep about the same time. I had gone to sleep, and that same bright light was shining again on my face. But this time, it had similar rings around the white light, starting with light brown, gradually getting dark brown to the dark surroundings. It was the same light, same shading around the light.

But this time, the light didn't stay at the same intensity as the last time. This time, it seems to glow brighter and then with lower power. It was like a candle flickering. After a while, I opened my eyes, and the bedroom was dark, and the clock said twelve thirty. Again, I sat up in bed to ponder on what I saw.

It was like the Holy Spirit showing His tender heart, longing for me. He has a soft, tender heart, never pushy, never rough, but a gentle touch. That's why He seems to grieve the minute I take my eyes off Him, of the Father, of Jesus. He grieves when my heart goes away for other stuff, other temptations, other desires away from Him. He is tender, never pushes me. But He longs for me, and He always fixed His eyes on me, so He wants the same from me; that my eyes should have them set on Him.

As He said, his desire for me also, "Beloved, you prosper and be in good health as your soul prospers" (3 John 1:2).

He wants good things for me, a good future for me.

Jesus took stripes for me so I could be healed.

He wants me to be healed because He already paid the price for me, not only for my salvation, my sins forgiven, but also for my healing so I can rise up and walk. He that is in me than greater than He that is in the world.

"Lord, I want to receive it and take it from You. All I need is a mustard seed faith, strong bulldog faith. My heart's desire should be the same desire You have for me. I am Yours, and You are mine. I should not vex or sadden You in anything I do. You have sealed me, marked me, branded me as His own, secured for the day of redemption. What comfort You have sealed me, what a privilege that You have focused Your eyes on me, may I never hurt You in any way or anything I do. I love You so, so much. Lord, You have shown me the Bright Morning Star, Jesus to me, that my Spirit screamed out, 'I love You, Jesus,' then love of the Father and the love of the Holy Spirit showed up in yearnings for me because I shouted, 'I love You, Jesus.' Oh, what love beyond measure, You are to me. Take me as an offering, as a living sacrifice, in my Jesus's precious name, amen and amen!"

He helps me in my weakness; He prays to the Father for me with groanings that I cannot understand, but my Father knows and causes everything to work together for good as I love Him so much.

> *In the same way, the Holy Spirit [comes to us and] helps us in our weakness. We do not know what prayer to offer or how to offer it as we should, but the Spirit Himself [knows our need and at the right time] intercedes on our behalf with sighs and groanings too deep for words. And He who searches the hearts knows what the mind of the Spirit is, because the Spirit intercedes [before God] on behalf of [a] God's people in accordance with God's will.*
>
> *And we know [with great confidence] that God [who is deeply concerned about us] causes all things to work together [as a plan] for good for those who love God, to those who are called according to His plan and purpose.* (Romans 8:26–28 Amp.)

> *The Holy Spirit of God has sealed you in Jesus Christ until you experience your full*

salvation. So never grieve the Spirit of God
or take for granted his holy influence in your
life." (Ephesians 4:30 Passion)

The four dreams above said so many things to me this year that in a matter of days, weeks, and months, Jesus appeared to me in my Spirit; only my Spirit could see Him. He was too bright for my physical eyes to see. God, the Father, showed me how much love He had for me—so much love that I could feel the warm hugs and His kisses on my cheeks I could never forget. And the Holy Spirit, with His bright blinding eye, focused on me that He has sealed me forever and how He longs for me through thick and thin. I never want to grieve Him; he is so tender, meek, never forceful, and never waver in His love for me. May I never be a moment away from His love and fellowship but ever so be closer drawn to Him moment by moment, even as my soul prospers in Him. May I ever live to please Him.

May the grace of the Lord Jesus the Anointed,
the love of God the Father,
and the fellowship of the Holy Spirit
remain with you all. Amen. (2 Corinthians 13:14)

23

Angels Dancing and Rejoicing

Night of October 30, 2015

That evening, I was listening to a pastor talking about angels. I got very curious. That night, as I was going to sleep, I asked Jesus to lift me in the spirit world and see angels. I went to sleep, and then I saw in the darkness angel or angels coming down. They were white images in a dark background. Then as they came in front, it was as if they were falling; they were turning and twisting in front. What I saw was not too clear. It was as if I was looking through a haze. I could not really figure out what I saw. I was wondering what they were doing; I just wondered what was going on.

I asked the Lord to discern whether it was from Him. Then the whole scene disappeared. So I was puzzled.

I did not open my eyes but had my eyes closed, but as I was still thinking of what I saw, I went back to sleep.

So God answered my request to see angels, and I was thankful, but I could not understand what went on. So I was asking the Lord, in the next few nights, specifically one night, I asked Jesus again, can I see the angels in a more precise form and see what they were doing? Then, I went to sleep. Sometime that night, I saw on a screen in front, angels came down, this time more clearly, and started to dance before me. They were all in white, and they did have enormous wings behind them. But I could not see their faces. So what I saw was similar to the last time before, all the twisting and turning of the angels, that they were dancing. It looked like they were having a party; it lasted for quite a while. So even the time before, it was a party, but it was much clearer this time than the last time. But both times, they were dancing and having a big party as well.

In the morning, I was thinking why were always dancing. Then the following verse came, "That's the way God responds every time one lost sinner repents and turns to him. He says to all his angels, 'Let's have a joyous celebration, for that one who was lost I have found!" (Luke 15:10 PI).

In this world, with over 7.8 billion population, there is always at least one sinner coming to know Jesus, every second, every minute, and repenting. So in heaven, there is an outburst of joy. But every time, which has become constant, angels are always rejoicing, joy is overflowing. So when they rejoice, there is a party. Just like the prodigal son came home, the Father wanted to throw a big party, and so they are rejoicing and dancing. Maybe the angels take turns. Can I also rejoice and dance that someone is always coming to know the Lord? That's wonderful. That's incredible.

Do I want to rejoice? Do I want to see people coming to know the Lord? Do I want to see prodigal sons come back to the Heavenly Father?

I was reading a story where the disciples left Jesus alone by a well to get lunch. Below is the story in the Bible, in John, chapter 4:6 to 27 (ERV).

> *It was about noon. A Samaritan woman came to the well to get some water, and Jesus said to her, "Please give me a drink." This happened while his followers were in town buying some food.*

The woman answered, "I am surprised that you ask me for a drink! You are a Jew and I am a Samaritan woman!" (Jews have nothing to do with Samaritans.)

Jesus answered, "You don't know what God can give you. And you don't know who I am, the one who asked you for a drink. If you knew, you would have asked me, and I would have given you living water."

The woman said, "Sir, where will you get that living water? The well is very deep, and you have nothing to get water with. 12. Are you greater than our ancestor Jacob? He is the one who gave us this well. He drank from it himself, and his sons and all his animals drank from it too."

Jesus answered, "Everyone who drinks this water will be thirsty again. But anyone who drinks the water I give will never be thirsty again. The water I give people will be like a spring flowing inside them. It will bring them eternal life."

The woman said to Jesus, "Sir, give me this water. Then I will never be thirsty again *and won't have to come back here to get more water."*

Jesus told her, "Go get your husband and come back."

The woman answered, "But I have no husband."

Jesus said to her, "You are right to say you have no husband.

That's because, although you have had five husbands, the man you live with now is not your husband. That much was the truth."

The woman said, "Sir, I can see that you are a prophet.

Our fathers worshiped on this mountain. But you Jews say that Jerusalem is the place where people must worship."

Jesus said, "Believe me, woman! The time is coming when you will not have to be in Jerusalem or on this mountain to worship the Father. You Samaritans worship something you don't understand. We Jews understand what we worship, since salvation comes from the Jews. But the time is coming when the true worshipers will worship the

Father in spirit and truth. In fact, that time is now here. And these are the kind of people the Father wants to be his worshipers. God is spirit. So the people who worship him must worship in spirit and truth."

The woman said, "I know that the Messiah is coming." (He is the one called Christ.) "When he comes, he will explain everything to us."

Then Jesus said, "He is talking to you now—I am the Messiah."

Just then Jesus' followers came back from town. They were surprised because they saw Jesus talking with a woman. But none of them asked, "What do you want?" or "Why are you talking with her?"

Then the woman left her water jar and went back to town. She told the people there, "A man told me everything I have ever done. Come see him. Maybe he is the Messiah."

So the people left the town and went to see Jesus.

While the woman was in town, Jesus' followers were begging him, "Teacher, eat something!"

But Jesus answered, "I have food to eat
that you know nothing about."

So the His disciples asked themselves,
"Did someone already bring him some food?"

Jesus said, "My food is to do what the
one who sent me wants me to do. My food
is to finish the work that he gave me to do."

As a result, that whole town of Samaria
came to know and follow Jesus.

That day, there was the biggest party that went on heaven—angels dancing and rejoicing! And Jesus told the disciples, His food was His satisfaction in knowing they found salvation. And His happiness came when He was able to tell a whole town that He came to save them. He was so happy.

So after this dream, I have asked Jesus, "Lord, give me those days, that I can dance and rejoice with angels because of what I do. I want to be constantly in tune with You, that I can be good to people, love them so much, that they may come to know You, because of my love for them, and You, that they can come to love You too. Please forgive me if I let You down. Fill me with love, joy, peace, kindness, goodness, and gentleness.

Can I pray for them? Can I do something for them?

Can I write to them, or can I say or speak anything that comforts them? Make me a blessing for You to them, in whatever way; make me do anything that will show Your love for them, so that they may come to know You and love You too.

I want them to enjoy the same happiness You have given me and rejoice in the same goodness I have with You and from You, the same blessings You have poured on my life.

So as they come to know You, as You and Angels have the party, that I too can join You, dancing the night away!

In Jesus's Name, I ask You with thanksgiving. Amen!

"A merry heart does good like a medicine" (Proverbs 17:22 KJV).

24

Miracle at Yosemite

It was September 2014 that our group of international students decided to go to Yosemite. A church in Mariposa would welcome international students, host them for the weekend, and take them to Yosemite National Park. We had gone there once before in the spring, and they took us to the different Falls in the Yosemite Valley; this church entertained us, and we had a great time when we had gone before.

So we had arranged with this church again for them to host us for a weekend. We were to leave Huntington Beach early Friday morning with a large van full of international students and some cars and head out to Yosemite. The students came from China, Japan, S. Korea, Indonesia, Palestine, India, Vietnam, Thailand, Cambodia, etc.

Not sure exactly how many students were there, but there were approximately twenty students plus volunteers. The program was to leave Friday morning from Huntington Beach, pick up students on the way, stop somewhere for lunch and keep heading to Redwood Grove in Yosemite National Park before sunset and spend some time at the Grove enjoying its beauty. Then get some dinner and get to the church hosting us by 8:30 or 9:00 p.m. that evening, spend the evening with different families, and spend the night.

Then Saturday morning, the families provided breakfast for the students and volunteers, me being one of them and taking them to church by 9:00 a.m. on Saturday. Then the students were to be placed with church members in their cars and taken to Yosemite Sentinel Dome.

This time being the beginning of September, we drove up to the upper part of Yosemite Park overlooking the whole valley, being about six thousand to seven thousand feet in elevation. Then spend the entire Saturday at various locations of the upper Yosemite. We were going to start with Sentinel Dome and then head to Glacier Point, overlooking Half Dome. Then evening, come back to town, have dinner, spend the night with families, go to church Sunday morning, have lunch and drive back home.

We had let the students know about this trip for about two to three months before the students, and we were signing them in and paying their deposits. Most of them have never been to Yosemite, and they were getting excited. The cost was meager since there was no cost for lodging and some food.

The students had heard about Yosemite from some of their friends, and some had seen the pictures of the falls, half dome, from Google. They were all looking forward to going there. And few of them had been to Yosemite Valley and had seen the falls but never been to the Upper Yosemite Sentinel Dome. So Friday morning, we all left in one big van and few cars and headed for the park. It was about a six-to seven-hour drive, but with the breaks, it was even longer.

As we were driving, the weather was a little overcast but still good. I had never looked at the weather forecast for the weekend at Yosemite. Usually, September is still warm, and we didn't expect any cold weather to come on, but I decided to see the forecast. It forecasted for the whole Saturday for Yosemite, heavy rain turning into snow later that evening and night, becoming lighter on Sunday. I looked at various weather stations, and all of them showed the same. And I realized that Saturday is when we spend all day on Upper Yosemite Park. I was alarmed it forecasted heavy rain and snow. And I told that to Jim Easton, who was driving. Even though it was middle September, we had looked earlier that week, it had not forecasted rain or snow, and we had not checked later that week. We knew it was going to be cold but not a downpour of rain.

I remembered the passage from James 5:16b and 17 (NKJV): "The effective, fervent prayer of a righteous man avails much. Elijah was a man with a nature like ours, and he prayed earnestly that it would not rain, and it did not rain on the land for three years and six months."

That verse just riveted me. It said Elijah was a man with a nature like me and all he did was pray an effective, fervent prayer. So can I pray an effective, fervent prayer and earnestly plead with God for the rain and snow to stop? If Elijah prayed and made God stop the rain for three and a half years, can I not ask God to stop it for ten hours for all the students who have been dreaming for days, weeks, and even years to enjoy Yosemite?

So I took my request to the Lord, "Lord, these are students visiting from all other countries, and they have been looking forward to this one day for weeks, maybe months, and some maybe even years to see one of the wonders of the world. Just like Elijah, who had nature like me, God's Word says, he prayed fervently, effectively, for Israel to turn to You, can I not pray for these international students to enjoy that one day, they came to enjoy all the beauty You created in nature in Yosemite? Will You not stop this rain and snow or even postpone this rain and snow for ten hours, just ten hours, so the students can enjoy all You have created for us to enjoy Your beauty in creation? Just this one request to You created the heavens and the Earth, and You have the power. I come just like Elijah, just as I am, to You in Jesus's name. I worship You in Spirit and truth. I thank and praise You for who You are. You are a merciful and loving Father. In Jesus's name, I ask and pray!"

I prayed and left it to God because His Word says, in 1 Peter 5:7 (TLB), "Let Him have all your worries and cares, for He is always thinking about you and watching everything that concerns you." Once I prayed and left it in God's hand, I went back to talking to the students. That evening we were at the Redwood Grove at Yosemite, and we had a great time. The students enjoyed the vast redwoods and took many pictures; some even ran around like little kids. It was a lot of fun.

Then we went to the church, met all the families there to meet them. Then the families took three or four students each, along with the volunteers to various homes. It was interesting that nobody talked about the weather forecast, and I didn't either. I had given my request to the Lord, and He was going to take care of it.

The following day we all woke up, and again, it was overcast like the previous day. The students enjoyed staying with the families. For some students, this was the first experience of staying with an American family. They enjoyed being with the little kids in their homes, talking and playing with them, and had a great time.

Then we all headed out to church to get our winter gear for the students who didn't come prepared for the cold because we would be at six thousand to seven thousand feet in altitude. The sky was still overcast, but neither rain nor snow had appeared. My heart was still in a prayerful mode. And my faith was in my Savior, Jesus. Some of the leadership in the church were talking about the forecast, but I didn't get into their conversation. I didn't want to get into doubts when my faith was in my Savior.

The ride to Yosemite Sentinel Dome was beautiful, and the students were enjoying the scenery. It was still only overcast, and there were not threatening black clouds, and my faith got strengthened. The forecast had predicted heavy rain starting overnight. "Lord, thank You for answering me. Thank You, Lord, for holding back the rain even this morning. My faith is in You. As I believe in You and Your promises, I know You will come through for me this whole day. In Jesus's precious name."

I also trusted Mark 11:24, which read, "Therefore I tell you, whatever you ask for in prayer, believe that you have received it, and it will be yours." These were Jesus's words, so I asked, believing I have received what I asked, and what I asked, it will be mine.

So we got to Sentinel Dome, and all the students got off the cars and went on a short hike up to the top of the Dome. It was cold, but all the students were dressed for the cold. It was still only overcast but no rain or dangerous black clouds. The students were running all over the Dome, looking to various viewpoints, having a great time. All of them had their cameras out as well as their phones and taking pictures.

About half an hour after we arrived, we started seeing small snow flurries. Then some of the flurries got mixed with bigger ones but only snow flurries. They were so light that in the light wind, they were dancing all over the air. And as they landed on one's hand, it was a beautiful snowflake, so lovely to behold. None of the students have seen this before, so they were all so excited. They were having a great time. This went on for an hour or two, and the students were having such a wonderful time, enjoying something they have never seen before.

My heart was so full of joy that God not only answered my prayer by stopping the rain and snow but gave a great gift of snowflakes that students enjoyed and having such a great time. Later on, the snow flurries stopped, but the beautiful sun showed up. Then it got warmer and turned out to be a beautiful day. My heart was praising the Lord, that He answered my prayer beyond belief. It was a miracle indeed!

That whole day, we were in the Upper Yosemite looking at the Half Dome, the Yosemite Valley, so many falls from the top, the Yosemite Falls, Vernal Falls, Nevada Falls, and other ones we could see with telephoto lens. That was such a great day.

The sun was bright the whole afternoon. The about 5:30 p.m., we all got into various cars to go back to where we were staying; just as we were driving out, just a heavy downpour of snow came down. All the students who had never seen snow before rolled down the car windows, stuck out their hands to feel and touch and enjoy the snow.

I have posted the pictures of this trip with the students as well—what a day that was and how God was faithful to my simple request. Yes, Elijah was able to stop the rain for three and a half years, but to me, when God stopped the snow and the rain for ten hours, that was such a great answer; more than I received, I was so thankful and grateful to the Lord. I was singing this song on the way home.

> Oh Lord My God, when I in Awesome Wonder,
> Consider all the worlds Thy hands have made;
> I see the stars, I hear the rolling thunder,
> Thy power throughout the universe displayed.
> Then sings My soul, My Savior God, to Thee,
> How great Thou art! How great Thou art!
> Then sings My soul, My Savior God, to Thee,

How great Thou art! How great Thou art!
And when I think, that God, His Son not
sparing;
Sent Him to die, I scarce can take it in;
That on the cross, My burden gladly
bearing,
He bled and died to take away My sin.
When through the woods, and forest
glades I wander,
And hear the birds sing sweetly in the
trees.
When I look down, from lofty mountain
grandeur
And hear the brook, and feel the gentle
breeze.
Then sings my soul…

25

Showing of Things Yet to Come

Even though I started as an architectural designer, I got into construction, real estate development, project management, and various facets related to architecture. Different circumstances brought about changes in what I did, and then, I got into commercial real estate about four years ago. I always worked with so many clients and other professionals that my new occupation helped my previous clients and new ones. Even as I got together with them, they knew my previous background and knew I could help them.

I found a new client that got into real estate development, and we got along well. He wanted to find sites for him to develop apartments in the right parts of Los Angeles. In March of 2019, I found him a site he liked, and I started working on it. It already had most of the approvals in process, and he started getting into the details of whether it had all the approvals. This project was getting approved for sixty-three units and six thousand square feet of retail on the street level; it was seven stories tall, about a mile away from downtown Los Angeles. The city of Los Angeles is extensive, and so were a large planning staff and a lengthy approval process.

This project was in the last two to three months getting all the approvals. My client got into a contract with the seller and in the process was a commission for me. As an architect, I was able to help my client, and we got along great. He was appreciative of what I knew. But soon after he got into contract, my client found out that the seller had obtained approvals only for architectural and structural drawings but not the other disciplines like mech., plumbing, etc. Since he had a short escrow, he was in a pickle about how he can get all other disciplines approved before he closed escrow. He was unsure whether he should go ahead with his contract since it had a short fuse or cancel. It was unknown whether this escrow will likely close. I took this to the Lord and was relying on 1 Peter 5:7 (NKJV), "Casting all your care upon Him, for He cares for you."

I knew my firm's head about twenty-five years ago when we were neighbors and became good friends. One day, I told him about our project's ordeals, and he got interested in this project. He was the one that introduced me to my client for another project, and I have gotten to know this client well. He wanted to learn more, and I told him all that I knew. Then whenever I met him at the office, we would talk about what was going on.

About a month after we got into escrow on that project, one morning, as I was meditating on a verse in my quiet time with my Lord, as I had closed my eyes, I saw big numbers in the thousands in front on a white background. It was there for quite some time, and then another set of numbers appeared. This was also there for quite a while. Then, I opened my eyes, and both those numbers stuck in my mind. As I was thinking about it, I realized the first set of numbers was my commission check. I was in awe of why they appeared. Then the second set of numbers was what I had in my Bank account at that time.

It was bizarre, I thought. These two numbers, I knew, but why together? I had not thought about these numbers for a long time. Those numbers appeared big, and they were very unusual. I pondered whether the Lord was telling me something, being so vivid in my mind.

A few days later, I was reading John 16, and then I read in verse 13, "However, when the Spirit of Truth comes, He will guide you into all truth. He will not speak of His own. He will speak only what He hears, and He will tell you what is yet to come." I thought about those numbers, and I asked the Lord, "Are You telling me, Lord, one is yet to come? Is it going to happen?" Those two numbers, one after the other was very mysterious. I thanked the Lord, and I kept it in the back of my mind. One was there in my bank, and the other is one yet to come?

Shortly, we had a meeting at the site with my client, the seller, and his agent. The meeting went well. My buyer found out the seller also was a contractor, and my client asked if the seller may be able to act as the contractor on this project and whether he would give him an estimate. So both agreed, which was a positive step.

My client was also trying to arrange his funding for construction and worked at several different sources, both for construction and equity. He was having difficulties and looked like the project may fall apart at any time at various points. In the meantime, the seller's agent was pushing my client to commit to close the escrow. My client kept postponing committing.

I approached the head of our company and arranged a meeting arranged between him and my client. That meeting went well, and the head of our company said he could place the needed financing for both the equity portion and the debt side. Initially, it was supposed to close in three months, but it pushed for a few more months. There were several hiccups, but finally, it was getting close to finalizing all documentation with the financing arranged. My office manager was arranging for my commission to be part of the disbursement. It was the number as was in the original agreement.

The next day, my office manager came and told me that there was a new agreement between the buyer and seller, and I would be getting less commission and gave me the amount I would get. It surprised me, and then I realized it was less than what I had seen before in my quiet time. I asked the Lord whether what He had shown me in my quiet time was wrong and asked for clarity. Another verse came up. "Ask me, and I will tell you remarkable secrets you do not know about things to come" (Jeremiah 33:3 NLT).

God said, "Ask me, and I will tell you…about things to come." Again, I went to the Lord and asked Him, "Lord, You showed me the numbers in my quiet time. However, what my manager is telling me is different and less. I will leave it all in Your hands. I know You care for me."

The escrow was set to close in about five days, but the day before it closed, my office manager came back to me and told me that my commission got changed again and is going to be the original amount, not what she told me three days before. It gave me a reminder that God is faithful to what He promised. As I asked Him, He came through just as He promised. I was so grateful to the Lord that His Word and His promises are true. The project finally closed. Again, God had come through. Because of this commission, we could buy a house closer to our kids, and so many beautiful things have happened since then.

This showed the faithfulness of God in my life. God had confirmed what He was going to give me. It was incredible how it came as promised. It reminded me of a verse in 2 Corinthians 4:18, "So we do not look at what we can see right now, the troubles all around us, but we look forward to the joys in Heaven which we have not yet seen. The troubles will soon be over, but the joys to come will last forever."

If He had not shown me, what I was to get, I would have been looking at all the troubles facing escrow instead of what He showed me is ahead. I was able to look forward to the escrow closing. Now the Word of God can show me the promises and what is ahead to look forward toward the heavenly journey. Especially the Book of Revelations can show me what to look forward to, the joys of heaven, which we have not yet seen. What we read about heaven is only limited to our imagination in what we read. When we see heaven in reality, it will be much bigger, grander, and more beautiful than our most incredible imagination, and our joys will last forever; it will never end. What a great promise, that promise is bound to happen.

Another verse, 2 Corinthians 1:20, "For all the promises of God in Him are Yes, and in Him Amen, to the glory of God through us."

All of God's promises are resounding "yes" and "amen." God's love for me now is far beyond my wildest imagination. "Rejoice in the Lord always, and again I say, Rejoice" (Philippians 4:4 JUB).

Even though I may now see only the troubles around me, and even though I do not know what He has planned for me, I do look forward to, are the joys of heaven and rejoice. These promises are "yes" and "amen"; they are bound to happen. Yes, one day, I will be soaking in the joys of heaven. "Yea, yea, yea!"

26

Even In London, My Wallet!

One city I love is London, and it was a treat to visit in September 2021. Our son, his wife, and his son were in Kenya for five years and were thinking of moving back to the US, and he asked his company about it. Their headquarters were in London. They replied to him, saying that he could move to London. So he decided to take that offer and move to London.

My son and his wife both worked in Kenya, and they had a nanny to look after their two-year-old son. But in London, nannies were expensive. So they asked us if we would come to London for one month and babysit. That was a dream come true. First, we had not seen our two-year-old grandson for over a year. Second, London was my dream city, and that request was a dream come. And so we left.

We got there at about the same time they got there. When we saw our grandson, he was so excited and came to hug us. We had not physically seen him for over a year, and even though we had seen him over the iPhone, we didn't know whether he would throw a tantrum over coming over to us. But we were thrilled that he was so excited to come to us.

I had been to London many times, yet it was so exciting. I landed in London and stayed for seven weeks when I first left India. Even though it had been so many years, London had not changed much. There was so much new construction everywhere, but London was still the same. So much was built over the centuries, but the classic London was still the same. One could still see the same architecture—Gothic, Renaissance, Victorian, Baroque, Roman, contemporary, and modern. That was the headquarters for James Bond, Agent 007. They were all a treat to my eyes. I was thanking my Lord for the feast He was giving me and my eyes.

Along with taking our grandson to the beautiful parks there, my great pastime was to get into the double-decker bus, climb up to the second story, try to get into the front seat, and feast my eyes on all the architecture I saw. And my iPhone was busy taking all the pictures it wanted to take. By the end of the day, the iPhone battery was depleted. Sometimes, just for the fun of it, we would take the bus and go from one end to the other, just watching all the scenes go by. Another fun thing to do was visit the various markets and parks around London. They were all so different, and there were so many exciting shops and unusual varieties of things one could buy.

One day, as I was getting off the bus and walking to my son's home, I realized my wallet was missing. When I got on the bus, I did take my Visa card and paid for the ticket. I had almost reached his home when I realized it was not in my pocket. I called my wife, and she asked me to retrace my steps. So I ran back to where I had gotten off the bus, my eyes wandering back and forth on the sidewalk in case I had dropped it there. Then it was my prayer to my Lord, asking whether He can show it to me. I reached where I had gotten off the bus, but there was no sign of it. I stood there at the bus stop, but no sign of my wallet anywhere. I was aghast.

In chapter 1, I remembered as a young man when I lost my suitcase on the way to Nasik in India for a camp. How lonely I felt. All my clothes, money, and belongings were gone, and it looked like I was so alone even when surrounded by so many friends. I had felt so lost and so lonely. How the thought that I had only one set of clothes I wore for three weeks, no money and nothing else. But then all the

Bible verses had come to my mind—verses that said that no matter how lonely I was, Jesus was next to me, that He was all that I needed, and that He was everything to me.

To me, this wallet was so minuscule compared to my suitcase, and I still had Jesus all along, and when He is everything to me, why should I be so worried. It was sad, but nothing mattered. Christ was all that mattered. I called my wife, told her what had happened, and headed back to my son's home. Yes, I lost my wallet, driver's license, Visa cards, debit cards, dollar bills, British Pounds, etc. But I had Jesus in my heart.

> *The Lord is my shepherd; I have all that I need. He lets me rest in green meadows; he leads me beside peaceful streams. He renews my strength. He guides me along the right paths, bringing honor to his name. Even when I walk through the darkest valley, I will not be afraid, for you are close beside me. Your rod and your staff protect and comfort me.* (Psalm 23:1–4 NLT)

I can say, "Even though I lost my wallet, I will not be afraid, for You, my Jesus, for You are close beside me." I can say He was close beside me always, not even a daybreak, a minute, or a second was he away.

Another verse that really talked to me is in Habakkuk 3:17–19 (MSG) as below:

> *Though the cherry trees don't blossom*
> *and the strawberries don't ripen,*
> *Though the apples are worm-eaten*
> *and the wheat fields stunted,*
> *Though the sheep pens are sheepless*
> *and the cattle barns empty,*
> *Yet, I'm singing joyful praise to God.*
> *I'm turning cartwheels of joy to my Savior*
> *God.*
> *Counting on God's Rule to prevail,*
> *I take heart and gain strength.*
> *I run like a deer.*
> *I feel like I'm the king of the Mountain!"*

I can also say as below:

Though I lost my wallet,
And lost all my credit cards,
Though I am out my British Pounds

And my American Dollars,
Even though I lost my Driver's License
As well as my Architect's License,
Yet, I'm singing joyful praise to God,
I'm turning cartwheels of joy to my Savior God.
Counting on God's Rule to prevail, I
take heart and gain strength.
I still run like a deer,
I still feel like I'm the king of the Mountain!

Maybe you, too, can also use these two passages when you've lost something or when something is hurting you rejoice in the fact that you are counting on God's rule to prevail and gain strength.

But then I will still continue to sing my favorite song:

Why should I be so discouraged
Why should the shadows come,
Why should my heart be lonely
And long for heaven and home.
When Jesus is my portion
A constant friend is He
His eye is on the sparrow
And I know He watches over me

His eye is on the sparrow
And I know He watches over me.
I sing because I'm happy
I sing because I'm free
His eye is on the sparrow
And I know He watches over me,
He watches over me.

(Curtis B. Doss)

27

I Can Only Imagine!

A while ago, a couple from our church invited me to a Sunday school class for international students. I, being from India, was no longer a student but was curious and agreed to attend. After a while, the same couple invited my wife and me to attend a Friday night group for international students at their house. They lived in a condo close to our house, and we started to attend. That Friday night group grew to over twenty to twenty-five, and their condo proved to be too small.

At that time, we had a relatively large home, and that couple asked us whether we would be open to having that Friday night group in our home for that summer. That summer became more or less permanent because the group grew to be forty students, fifty, and then sixty. Then at Christmas party, over one hundred students turned up.

The students came from various countries, and every year, the students changed; sometimes half the group stayed but it varied. We would always provide dinner, and whether it was thirty or sixty, there was always enough food to eat for everyone; it was like the miracle of the loaves with Jesus in our midst. We had moved houses, but we still had the Friday night group held in our home. It is hard to mention all that happened, but some interesting and funny things happened along the way.

One New Year's Eve, we planned to have a party. It was a fun night playing games till midnight. We all planned to stay awake till midnight, greet each other for the New Year, then all go to sleep. Everyone slept mainly in the living room, either on sleeping bags or the carpeted floors, got up about 5:30 a.m., got dressed up, and headed for the Rose Parade in Pasadena. Everything was going as planned, and there were about fifty to sixty students to my remembrance. And one of the leaders, an ardent hiker, stood and asked whether the students would be interested in a night hike after midnight. A lot of students thought that it was very adventurous and said they would be interested.

About twenty students raised their hands. So I told them if they were going, they should all come back before

5:30 a.m., so we could all go as a group to Rose Parade. They all agreed. So the midnight hour came, and we all greeted each other, and the group of twenty students left for the night hike. The rest of us got into bed, turned off the lights, and went to sleep. We left the front door open so the twenty night hikers could get back and get in the house.

My daughter had gone for the New Year's Eve party and came back after we had all gone to sleep. She didn't know anything about twenty night hikers and locked the front door behind her. All the twenty night hikers came back about 4:00 a.m., cold and shivering, wanting to get back to the house's heat. But when they tried to open the door, thinking it would be open, they found it locked. Then they frantically rang the doorbell. But everyone inside was so sound asleep, and nobody got up to open the door for them. So the gang of twenty had to stand up in the cold outside, still shivering. The alarm inside rang at 5:30 a.m., and someone inside switched on the living room light.

The gang of twenty saw the light inside and madly rang the doorbell, and finally, the door opened. Then it was time to get dressed, get into the cars, and head to the Rose Parade. The twenty did not get any sleep at all, started to sleep in the cars on the way to the Rose Parade. But that was only like foty minutes. Then there was a long walk to find a place to sit and watch the parade. It was still cold. But we had to carry all the chairs and other goodies like food, blankets, etc., to where we were seated. So finally, we found a place to sit at about 7:30 a.m. And the parade started at about 8:30 a.m.

But the twenty, after they got the seats, all went to sleep because they never got any sleep at night and were all so tired. So the parade came; and we all, including the thirty, enjoyed the parade but the twenty were sound asleep during the whole parade. We never could ask the twenty night hikers how the night hike was because they were sound asleep. These are some of the fun things that happened during the years of our international student meetings in our house.

We had to change our house again, and all our leadership changed as well as the students. One of the students who started coming was a Chinese student named Christophe, born in Belgium but moved to Surinam with his mom but came to the US to study. He was attending Rancho Santa Ana College. He became a regular attendee, and he came with his mom. At the time, my wife had started to work, and she had to get up at 5:00 a.m. to get dressed for work; she told me and the group she could not cook anymore or may not stay till we finished because she got up early and was getting tired.

Christophe came to me and volunteered, telling me that he could cook for our group. That was a great relief to me, and I thanked him for coming in the time of need. So he was faithful, and we always had meals every Friday. Sometimes, his mom would cook as well. Christophe studied here for four years and got his bachelor's at Cal State Fullerton. Then he told me he tried to get his funds for doing his master's at Cal State, but the fees were high, and he could not get his funding to do his master's.

Then he told me because he was born in Belgium, he was considered a member of the EU; and he was able to get a free scholarship at the University of Oxford in England, and he was going there. He was going to study to get his master's degree in Bbioinformatics. Then he and his mom left for the UK, and we missed them.

After a couple of years, he came back to visit, and he and his mom were able to attend one of our international student trips to Lake Arrowhead. We had a great time. At that time, we had a cabin there, and we stayed for a long weekend where we went hiking, did some Bible studies, etc. It was good to see him again.

We kept in touch, and we missed him and his mom here. After a while, he told me he was getting married, and he invited us to his wedding. We accepted his invitation, and we went to Cambridge in the UK to attend his wedding. He made all the plans for us, and we had a great time at his wedding. We enjoyed seeing Cambridge too. A couple of our student leaders also participated in the wedding, and we had a wonderful time. Then as I kept in touch with Christophe, he told me that they had a son and then a daughter.

So when our son invited us to London for a month, this September, I wrote to Christophe whether we could visit him since he was living close to Cambridge, and he wrote back and said that we could stay with him for a few days since he had an extra bedroom and could stay at his house. They lived in a town called Cambourne, about ten miles from Cambridge. It was a treat to meet his family; his son is about five and his daughter about two. We stayed five days at his home, and he took the five days off from work. He and his wife took us to Cambridge for a day, spent the whole day there. Then the next day to Yarmouth, we went to where he owns a 16 key hotel, and his mom is managing the hotel. It was so good to see her too. We stayed one night at the hotel, which is about one hundred miles from where he lives. That hotel faces the ocean, and we had a room with an ocean view, quite a treat for us.

We went around Yarmouth, which is a beach town. There are casinos, arcades, and many restaurants as well, a boardwalk on the beach. He also took us to Norwich, close by a beautiful old city with a huge cathedral. We spent most of the day there, walking all the shopping alleys and malls, some of them very old and very beautiful. We also went to the beautiful cathedral and spent quite a while there, enjoying all the Gothic architecture with the stained glass windows and doors. Then he showed us the town he lives in, Cambourne; we went for a walk to a beautiful lake where swans were there. He told me they were involved in a church in Cambourne, with about twenty active members. He told me he meets with the Pastor regularly.

When I first met Christophe in our house, would I have known he would take his time off and drive us around to Cambridge, Norwich, and Yarmouth? I never knew he would start cooking when my wife could do it no longer.

I never knew he would invite me to his wedding, and we would have a great time in England. I could have never imagined he would take his time off to see all the great places and have such a good time, visiting places we had never seen. We got to enjoy his kids and had a wonderful time with his family, staying with them for five days. My years working with international students have paid me off more than I bargained for. God has given me back more than I can imagine.

> *Now to Him who is able to do immeasurably more than all we ask or imagine, according to His power that is at work within us, to him be glory in the church and in Christ Jesus throughout all generations, for ever and ever! Amen.* (Ephesians 3:20–21)

You might not be imagining when you come to know Jesus what glorious things you'll see even in the days to come, but when you go to heaven, you'll taste and see all the glorious things you'll never know or come across on the earth. You are a precious child of God. But you need to walk in the power of His love and the Holy Spirit. In heaven, all the things you will see and enjoy will be beyond your wildest imagination. Get prepared for it, and it will be way beyond what you can ask or think or imagine when you enter heaven and see Jesus.

I can only imagine
What it will be like
When that day comes
And I find myself standing in the Son
I can only imagine when all I would do
Is forever, forever worship You
I can only imagine, yeah

Surrounded by Your glory,
What will my heart feel?
Will I dance for you, Jesus?
Or in awe of You be still?
Will I stand in Your presence
Or to my knees, will I fall?
Will I sing hallelujah?
Will I be able to speak at all?
I can only imagine

I can only imagine
What it will be like
When I walk by Your side
I can only imagine

What my eyes would see
When Your face is before me
I can only imagine
Yeah...

(Jeff Carson/I Can Only Imagine)

28

House with Red Bougainvillea?

Last year, in April 2019, I went to sleep at bedtime. It was just like any other night; that night, I had a dream. I woke up the following day, and this dream was fresh in my mind, just like today. I was walking through a street, a new neighborhood, I saw walls on both sides, and I also saw red bougainvillea on top of the wall on the other side of the wall. I kept walking and looking at the beautiful red bougainvillea, and that was the end of the dream. I thought that was nothing unusual. When I woke up in the morning, that dream was very vivid in my mind. Later that day, I forgot that dream.

That night, I went to bed. That night I had the same dream again; I woke up in the morning, vividly remembering that dream. It was the same dream as the previous night. Again, that dream came fresh to my mind, the same walls and the same beautiful red bougainvillea on the other side of the wall. This time, I asked the Lord if He was saying something to me. Did I ask Him why the same dream exactly repeated itself? No verse came into my mind; I didn't get any clue of an answer from the Lord then. But these dreams were always in the back of my mind. But I do write all the dreams I get in my Word document as soon as they occur.

Few days went by, and I kept asking the Lord what He was trying to tell me—no answer. Then months went by. In the meantime, I was working on one of the big projects, selling; everything seemed to be coming together toward the closing of escrow. I also had another nudge from the Lord, saying it was going to close. So I was thanking the Lord, how He was working for the good, and how things were going.

This verse kept coming to my mind, "And, we know that all things work together for good to those who love God, to those who are the called according to His purpose" (Romans 8:28). And I kept thanking the Lord how all things were falling into pieces like the picture was getting completed in a jigsaw puzzle.

Three years before that, we had moved away from our two daughters. We used to be only ten minutes away before, and now we were about twenty-five to thirty minutes away. The traffic in between was getting much busier. Now we saw less and less of them, and we missed seeing our grand-kids. So we were wondering whether we could move back closer to them at all. So when the project was going well, and looked like it was going to close pretty soon. So the thought came to me that if the project does close, I would be able to move closer.

I brought that idea to Sujita, and first, she said let the project close. So I didn't press the idea much. But it has been months, and the dream came back to my memory. So I asked the Lord, "Lord, were you showing me twice the same wall with red bougainvillea? Was that because we will move to a house with bougainvillea?" A few days later, I was reading John 16:13 (NIV), "But when He, the Spirit of truth, comes, He will guide you into all the truth. He will not speak on his own; He will speak only what He hears, and He will tell you what is yet to come." I started meditating on the verse. It said The Holy Spirit would tell me what is yet to come. Then that dream came back alive, "Lord, were You showing me another house we are going to move to?" I felt maybe God was telling me what is yet to come, a house with red bougainvillea.

The project did close in August, and I did get a big commission check. Then I talked to my wife about whether we can start looking at houses closer to the kids. She agreed. Then another verse came to my mind, and this was in Isaiah 45:11, "For the Lord, the Holy One of Israel, and its Maker says this, 'Ask Me about the things to come concerning My sons,' Then I asked the Lord again, 'Lord, this is Your Word, can I ask You about the things to come?'" There was no answer but just peace.

We just went to a few open houses. We looked at what our house may sell for. We then talked to the kids. Finally, we agreed to meet with a couple of brokers to see what we can list our house for. Both the brokers were very close to the price that they thought they could list our home for. We looked at all the numbers, what we could sell for, what we could buy for, and all the numbers seem to work. So we decided to list with one of the brokers that our daughter and son-in-law knew. It was on a Tuesday.

That Saturday, we were supposed to fly to Germany, where my nephew's son was getting married. We had arranged this trip for about two months before that. We told the listing agent what our plans were, and he said not to worry. He said he would have the pictures taken of the house on Thursday, have the Brochure done by Friday, and have an open house that Saturday and Sunday.

Well, that Saturday came, the listing broker had done the brochure, which looked great; we got the house ready for the open house. Since our flight was not till that evening, we decided to look at some of the open houses in the afternoon. We went back to a house that we had seen before, which was a possibility, and we asked the kids to join as well. Everybody seemed to like the home, except this house had to have a lot of work to be done. Our question was with the house's price, and all the money we have to spend on it, can we afford it?

We left on the flight that evening, and we were stopping in Paris and meeting my nephews and families on the way to Germany. When we arrived in Paris on that Sunday afternoon, there was a text from my listing broker, "A couple had seen the house on the Saturday open house, and they were going to make an offer, and I should be looking for the offer in my email."

We were taken by surprise. The very first day, the house was listed that we were going to receive an offer? Surprise! A miracle! The following two days, we were in Paris. And we were going back and forth on our emails on their offer and our counter-offer. We agreed to all the terms, even though we were apart about six thousand miles. But now, we have to find another house close to where our daughters live, but we were out for two weeks at the wedding and travel. But the buyers agreed to give us time. But all these happened by the grace of God.

In my mind, my dream came back alive. Was that God showing me what to expect of what is yet to come. My thoughts went back to the house we had gone to twice. I imagined whether I saw any big bush of red bougainvillea in that house? I didn't remember seeing any. I asked the Lord whether it was the one or another one we hadn't seen. I asked Him for wisdom in picking the house.

The two weeks in Europe went fast. We had a great time. We traveled with my nephews and nieces and their families—incredible scenery, fabulous cities to visit. After Paris, we went to Amsterdam, Cologne, and Bremen, where the wedding was. All the towns were excellent, and we thoroughly enjoyed every place. And the wedding went off well. We had a great time as well, so many great things to see and enjoy.

Then we were back home, and now we had to decide on a house. We took the kids to see that house again and several other houses also. I was looking for a home with red bougainvillea, and I did not see any. But that was my secret, and I didn't tell anybody. But the house that we went to visit again and again kept dropping their prices too. I kept praying whether that was the house. So then decided to make a low offer to have funds to do all that needed to be done. And the seller came back with a hard to resist counter, so we agreed to it.

The buyer of our house was patient enough to wait, and God made it all possible. We closed the escrow on both houses in November 2019. Luke 1:37 "For nothing will be impossible with God!" If it was not for God to show me in those dreams, we might have never taken this step, or at least I would not have taken this step. If He had shown me the dream once, I would have dismissed it as a pure dream. But when He showed me the same dream twice, I said, He was trying to tell me something. And six months later, it happened. The other day, I was looking out of the family room; I see over our back wall a red bougainvillea above the wall, on the other side. There, it was my dream that had come true; what the Lord showed had come true.

Now we live closer to our kids and grandkids, only five to ten minutes. We have a swimming pool in our backyard, and we have a great time when they come and swim. Because of COVID, even our church had a baptism in our pool. And we had enough money to get all the repairs done and even get a new kitchen—glory be to God. He has a purpose in everything He does. Can we have an influence on our grandkids at this stage of their lives? Yes, we definitely do.

> *Live full lives, full in the fullness of God. God can do anything, you know—far more than you could ever imagine or guess or request in your wildest dreams! He does it not by pushing us around but by working within us, His Spirit deeply and gently within us.* (Ephesians 3:19p, 20 Message)

29

The Unseen

One of my friends from India once told me a story about one of his professors in Madras. The professor was an avid reader and used to take the electric train, along with the students. The train had eight stops between the time the professor boarded to where he got off. This trip took about forty-five minutes. As soon as the train started, the professor would begin reading. He used to count the eight stops even while he was reading and when he counted the eighth stop, he would stand up and get off the train. The last stop had a travel time of about fifteen minutes.

The train stopped as usual at the first seven stops one day, but it got a red signal to stop before the last stop in the middle of its route. The professor was so engrossed in his reading, he got up, walked out of doors (in Madras, the doors never close, they're always open), and fell off the train about six to eight feet into dirt and gravel. All the students ran out and picked him up; he was bleeding and was injured. He had been so engrossed in his reading, and he ended up falling off the train. The professor had become oblivious to the rest of the world.

After I heard this story, I was recollecting a similar instance in my life. I had gone to my grandson's baseball game. I went to sit on the bleacher to watch the game. I looked to see where the rest of the family was seated, and I saw them toward the top of the bleachers. So I headed to sit where they were and had to sit on the top-most bleacher. It was a good game, and I enjoyed all the enthusiasm throughout the game, and I enjoyed my time watching.

At the end of the game, I got up to walk out. The person in front of me got up in a jerky way, and I tried to avoid him coming at me, and I lost my balance, and I fell backward, from the top of the bleacher into the ground, where it was bare dirt. The fall was about six to seven feet, and I landed on the dirt entirely on my back. My lower back was the first to hit the ground. I just lay there. And my son-in-law, Brad, gave me a hand to pull me up. I took his hand, just jumped, and got up. He asked me how I felt. I said that I was okay. He was surprised, almost shocked. He said after that fall, was I all right? I told him yes, but no hurt, no pain, and told him I was myself surprised.

One verse came to my mind.

> *Because you have made the Lord, who is my refuge, Even the Most High, your dwelling place, No evil shall befall you, nor shall any plague come near your dwelling; For He shall give His angels charge over you, To keep you in all your ways. In their hands they shall bear you up, Lest you dash your foot against a stone.* (Psalm 91:9–12 NKJ)

That was it because I made the Lord, my refuge, I had Angels soft-landed me on the ground, that I was fine when I got up. It was good to know that the hand of the Lord is there to protect me; there is a guardian angel there to land me softly. What a deal! I can trust my Lord, and what a passage! What protection! What a guarantee! The unseen angel held out his arm for a soft landing?

Another story needs to be told!

> *Therefore, the King sent horses and chariots and a great army there, and they came by night and surrounded the city. And when the servant of the man of God arose early and went out, there was an army, surrounding the city with horses and chariots. And his servant said to him, "Alas, my master! What shall we do?"*
>
> *So Elisha answered, "Do not fear, for those who are with us are more than those who are with them." And Elisha prayed and said, "Lord, I pray, open his eyes that he may see." Then the Lord opened the eyes of the young man, and he saw. And behold, the mountain was full of horses and chariots of fire all around Elisha."* (2 Kings 6:14–17)

One needs to read the whole chapter 6 to get the entire story. From this passage, I understand there is an army of angels in chariots of fire protecting me. *The Unseen.* Do I know that? Yes, I do. Elisha said those that are with us are more than those who are with an enemy I face. So the phrase, "Do not fear!" I realized whatever challenges I face, in whatever circumstance, Jesus who said is always with me, along with His army of angels, in chariots of fire, guarding me, so I never, ever have to fear anything in whatever circumstances I am in! There is an unseen force of my angels, who are always seeing the face of God, who is ready to protect me! What a deal!

Jesus said, "See that you don't despise one of these little ones, for I tell you that in heaven their angels always see the face of my Father who is in heaven" (Matthew 18:10 WEB).

30

My Secret

"John, how are you? What are you up to this weekend?"

"Hey, Andy, it's good to hear from you. I was thinking about that, what do you have in mind?"

"Well, haven't got anything planned yet…may go fishing?"

John wasn't so sure when he answered, "Andy, I haven't done that for a long time. You know Andy, you are a very experienced fisherman, and I'm just an amateur."

"It's so relaxing, looking at all that water, waiting for the fish to take the bait, I enjoy fishing. That's why I go almost every Saturday. How about joining me?"

"Okay, Saturday it is. We are going fishing!"

"Thanks, John, even though you haven't gone fishing a long time, I'm telling you, you'll enjoy it."

Reluctantly John answered, "You know I'll have to look in my garage and search for my fishing rod. It must be rusty now, then for the icebox and all the gear that goes along with it."

Andy was excited, "Call me Friday if you need anything. I'll bring it with me on it Saturday. We could go to Pyramid Lake. I heard they just stocked the lake with trout. If that's okay, I can pick you up at around 8:00 a.m."

"Okay, that's a deal. See you Saturday."

Saturday came, and Andy was on time at John's house.

John was able to get all his gear together by the time when Andy picked him up. They got to the lake, picked a good spot, and sat reasonably close together so they could talk but yet at a distance, so they didn't tangle their lines. They started fishing, and reasonably soon, the experienced one, Andy, caught a big fish and placed it in an icebox he had bought with him. Soon after, John also caught a big fish, but then he unhooked it and threw it back into the lake.

"Wow! Hey, John, you hooked that big one. That's great. I guess it isn't big enough for you, so you had to throw it back."

"No, I'm just very picky, I guess."

Pretty soon, they were catching big fish, one after another. They were happily chatting, cracking jokes, and laughing away. Andy would get a big fish and throw it in his icebox, but John would throw all the big ones he caught back into the lake. He did this number of times. Andy was thinking, *What's wrong with him? Why is he throwing all those big, good-looking fish back?*

So after a while, Andy asked, "I don't understand, John. I've seen you catch some big fish, but you have been throwing all of them back into the water. What's going on?"

To which, John replied, "You know I'm amazed that I'm catching all the big fish. But at home, I checked, and I have only a small frying pan so, none of the ones that I caught can fit in that pan."

Losing all the big fish just because all he had was a small frying pan? I've done that myself. Like John, who was trying to look for a fish that would fit his frying pan, I'm looking for the solution to all my problems that fit what I think it should be—or maybe, looking for the answers in the wrong places. If there are no answers, then I can get into a very depressing mood. When I think I can't find any solutions to our problems, I get more and more into negative thoughts. All I can think of is the pain, the hurt, and the issues that I am going through and nothing else.

Another way I found was to go to God, and instead of asking Him for what I need or what I want, is to give Him praise. It sounds strange, but I found God is a good God, who, when I praise Him, He loves to turn things for me even in the most challenging circumstances. I found the secret from a Bible story.

I was reading of the story of Paul and Silas in Acts, chapter 16, from verse 22 (Passion).

> *A great crowd gathered, and all the people joined in to come against them. The Roman officials ordered that Paul and Silas be stripped of their garments and beaten*

with rods on their bare backs. After they were
severely beaten, they were thrown into prison;
the jailer placed them in the innermost cell
of the prison and had their feet bound and
chained.

We don't know two thousand years ago what the prison conditions were, whether rats were running around or how hard and cold and creepy the prison floors were, whether they were sitting with their feet being bound and chained; they had been stripped of their clothes; they may also have bleeding from the earlier beating received on their bare backs, as well as from the chains were tied to. Undaunted, they prayed in the middle of the night and sang songs of praise to God while all the other prisoners listened to their worship.

So God heard them singing praises to Him by these two with their feet bound in chains, bleeding, with hardly any clothes on, being in the cold, while the others were listening to their worship. He got so happy with these two singing praises, despite their circumstances, and he enjoyed it so much; He started tapping His foot to the tunes these two were singing that it produced a great earthquake that shook the foundations of the prison. All at once, every prison door flung open, and the chains of all the prisoners came loose.

Startled, the jailer awoke and saw every cell door standing open. Assuming all the prisoners escaped, he drew his sword and was about to kill himself when Paul shouted in the darkness, "Stop! Don't hurt yourself. We're all still here." The jailer called for light. When he saw that they were still in their cells, he rushed in and fell, trembling at their feet. Then, he led them outside and asked, "What must I do to be saved?"

They answered him, "Believe in the Lord Jesus, and you will be saved, you and all your family." After he washed their wounds, he and his family were baptized. He took them to his home and set them at the table and fed them.

One can read what happened afterward. An unexpected earthquake happened when they sang praises to God amid their darkest days. Not only they came out of prison, but even the jailer and all his family were also filled with joy in their newfound faith in God. You and I, if we were thrown in prison and bound with chains, would we be singing praises to God or be crying with temper tantrums, "I am not guilty, get me out of here." Here was Peter and

Silas, being in the darkest day of their lives, were singing praises, having the time of their lives. God got so happy, so the unexpected happened.

In the first story, John was looking for a fish that fit into his pan, but in the second story, Peter and Silas were singing praises to God on the darkest day of their lives, so the unexpected happened. It is easy to be thankful and give praise when things are going good, but do I when things are tough? This has changed my thinking. Even though it may be challenging at first, may I learn to be like Peter and Silas, give praise, no matter what my circumstances may be, to God, who in turn could change things around for me for my good—unexpected, a suddenly moment happened.

In Genesis 50:20p, Joseph told his brothers, "As for you, you meant evil against me, but God meant it for good." When I praise God in all my circumstances, even when some plan evil against me, God is so good to turn things for me for my good and for many others that I could be a blessing as well. I may be in the middle of a wrong turn of events, but praise and adoration to my God can change any of my circumstances into an unexpected turn for my good. He can even create earthquakes to open the prison doors and change my circumstances into something good for me. This is my secret now. This will be a new paradigm for me and how much I enjoy being God's child!

> Oh, for a thousand tongues to sing
> My great Redeemer's praise
> The glories of my God and King
> The triumphs of His grace
> So come on and sing out
> Let our anthem grow loud
> There is one great love, Jesus
> Jesus, the name that charms our fears
> That bids our sorrows cease
> 'Tis music in the sinner's ears
> 'Tis life and health and peace
> He breaks the power of canceled sin
> He sets the prisoners free
> His blood can make the foulest clean
> His blood availed for me
> Glory to God and praise and love
> Be ever, ever giv'n
> By saints below and saints above
> The church in earth and Heav'n.
> (Charles Wesley)

31

Lost and Found

A few months ago, I had a dream that in my dream, I was wandering through the countryside; maybe it could have been a small town. My walk took me around some beautiful homes. The walk had some ups and downs. It was slowly getting dark. This was a late evening; the streets were not fully lit yet. As the sun was going down, the sky was red with few clouds. It was a gorgeous setting. I seemed to have been walking for quite a while.

As the sun was setting, the homes were getting beautifully lit, one at a time. I enjoyed my walk even in the dark, admiring all the houses and even the landscape around them. And all the lights, including some of the lights in the landscape, seem to twinkle. I was enjoying all that I saw, soaking it all. I kept walking and walking, didn't know for how long. That dream seemed so natural to me.

Then I remember walking across a very narrow trail, then on my right side seemed to have a sharp drop off, almost at the end of a cliff. And the path seemed to go on the incline. I saw no more homes, and now, it was getting dark. I didn't want to look down, to my right. Now, it was getting dark. I had to really watch my footsteps.

I remember carrying a backpack with some of its pockets being full but not fully zipped. My foot seems to hit a small stone at one point, and I seem to lose my balance and almost tripped. But I regained my balance, but the backpack being tossed; a couple of items seemed to have fallen off in the side of the deep cliff. I was stunned. After regaining my balance, I was even afraid to look down on what had fallen.

It was too dark even for me to check my backpack. But I kept walking the narrow trail, never minding what had fallen. After a while, the trail seemed to go lower and lower till I had hit a flat topo. The cliff came to an abrupt end, and I decided maybe I should walk back to where some of my items may have fallen. Even though it was pretty dark, I walked toward where I thought the things might have fallen.

As I was walking in total darkness, after a while, looking at the ground, I saw a key sticking out of the ground, shining like a bit of a twinkle. So as I went to pull it, a whole bunch of keys came out. They were all my keys, car key, house key, locker key, etc. And then not too far, was another twinkle, and that was my cell phone. I checked it, and it seemed to work fine. I looked up; the cliff could have been two hundred feet high. I was amazed, I found them all, even in the dark, and they all seemed to be okay. I thanked my God.

I proceeded to walk the path I had been walking. I came across a house fully lit, with lots of people. I went in and found I knew most of them, and that included some of my relatives. Then I proceeded to tell my story of how as I was walking by the side of the cliff, my keys and phone that fell from such a cliff about two hundred feet down, and I found it in darkness, but all that I had lost, survived the fall and came out intact.

I was so happy that I kept telling everyone, "It had to be God that showed me where my things fell. It had to be God." Everyone around me seemed to like what I had said and was very happy for me as well. I had tears of joy that I was able to share my happiness with my friends.

That's where the dream ended.

I think after a while, I woke up since I could still remember the dream, so vivid, it seemed so natural. Then I remembered the passage, Jesus was telling this parable below to His disciples.

> *Or what woman having ten pieces of silver, if she loses one piece, doth not light a lamp, and sweep the house, and seek diligently until she find it?*
>
> *And when she hath found it, she called together her friends and neighbors, saying, "Rejoice with me, for I have found the piece which I had lost."*
>
> *Even so, I say unto you, there is joy in the presence of the angels of God over one sinner that repents.* (Luke 15:8–10)

If I was so happy to find, what I lost, how much more, would God rejoice over you, God having compassion on you, having run toward you, who was once a prodigal son, and fell on your neck, and kissed you, for once you were lost but now am found. Do you know how precious you are to Him, when You turn to God either in a little thing or anything that has affected you, that You turn to God and ask His favor for You, how happy He is that You have looked to Him for His favor? When He is happy, the whole heaven rejoices, and You'll be happy to when He looks upon you with favor.

> *The Lord Your God is with you; His power gives you victory. The LORD will take delight in you, and in His love He will give you new life. He will sing and be joyful over you.* (Zephaniah 3:17 GNT)

Amazing Grace, How sweet the sound
That saved a wretch like me.
I once was lost, but now I am found,
Was blind, but now I see.
'Twas grace that taught my heart to fear,
And grace my fears relieved.
How precious did that grace appear
The hour I first believed.
Through many dangers, toils and snares
I have already come,
'Tis grace has brought me safe thus far
And grace will lead me home.
The Lord has promised good to me
His word my hope secures;
He will my shield and portion be,

As long as life endures.
Yea, when this flesh and heart shall fail,
And mortal life shall cease
I shall possess within the veil,
A life of joy and peace.
When we've been there ten thousand years
Bright shining as the sun,
We've no less days to sing God's praise
Than when we've first begun.
(John Newton)

32

How Incredible Heaven Will Be!

April 4, 2020

I woke up, and a dream that I dreamt either in the night or early morning came to my mind. I was in the woods, and I was with another friend. We were under a huge tree, and we proceeded to cross a large stream, but it was very shallow. The whole setting was beautiful. I jumped over rocks and crossed the creek. It was similar to many beautiful streams I had done hiking, in Idyllwild, in Lake Arrowhead, and so many other hikes I had gone on. I was on the other side of the creek, and I looked down the stream, and I saw a large log had fallen across the creek. I wondered whether I could cross back to the other side of the creek walking on the log.

That was all I could remember in the morning. So I started the quiet time. And this is the passage I saw in the Bible. Jesus was teaching the Lord's Prayer.

> *Now it came to pass, as He was praying in a certain place, when He ceased, that one of His disciples said to Him, "Lord, teach us to pray, as John also taught his disciples."*
> *So He said to them, "When you pray, say:*
> *Our Father]in Heaven,*
> *Hallowed be Your name.*
> *Your kingdom come.*
> *Your will be done*
> *On earth as it is in Heaven.* (Luke 11:1–2 NKJV)

Lord was praying, Your Kingdom come. Your will be done, on earth as in heaven. So to me in that dream, I was on earth, but it was as in heaven. Where I was there, it was so beautiful, and I could have spent my life in the woods. It was like being in heaven. I really enjoyed hiking. I enjoyed being in nature. The beauty was heaven on earth.

And I thought even though I don't go hiking that much anymore, not as much as I used to, I could go for hikes in heaven. Oh, what a thought!

I always wondered, when I go to heaven, it is eternity, so much time in my hands, what would I be doing? Now I know there will be forests in heaven, it will be beautiful, I can go hiking in heaven, I won't trip and fall, and even If I did, there would be an Angel to pick me up. I won't have any fear at all; even if a bear or lion appeared, it would be a friendly bear. It will greet me instead of chasing me. I will have all the time in heaven to enjoy nature. I can go camping for days, and there will be no time limit. So enjoying nature, I will be singing,

> When through the woods and forest glades
> I wander,
> And hear the birds sing sweetly in the trees,
> When I look down, from lofty mountain
> grandeur,
> And see the brook, and feel the gentle
> breeze.
> Then sings my soul, My Savior God to
> Thee,

> How great Thou art, How great Thou art,
> Then sings my soul, my Savior God to
> Thee,
> How great Thou art, How great Thou art.

What an incredible heaven that will be when I can wander through the forest, the shallow creeks, trees, and the beauty of nature. How I look forward to the day, I can wander with no time limit in mind. Earth, with the viruses, will be long gone, but heaven is waiting for me. Exploration of the forests in heaven is waiting for me!

"And God will wipe away every tear from their eyes; there shall be no more death, nor sorrow, nor crying. There shall be no more pain, for the former things have passed away" (Revelations 21:4 NKJV).

Another great news in heaven! I will never cry, I will never have dread death, neither grieve that someone close is dying, no more sorrow, no more sadness, no more COVID, no more pain, and nothing else to fear! No more loneliness, so many closes to me will be around me! Wow, I rejoice and dance now thinking of being heaven. That dream has made me sing and dance!

33

Breckenridge, a Glimpse of Heaven

In June 2020, we were in Breckenridge, Colorado. We had been planning this trip for about eight months, and then it happened. We weren't sure about the last three months with COVID-19, but everything worked together for good. And then we decided to go. The whole family went there; some went by plane, and some went by car. That entire week was amazing. On different days, we did various things.

We all were doing different things: horseback riding, biking, fishing, and hiking, and we were loving it all. We were laughing; we were having so much fun. We played cards and board games, swam in the pools they had, and enjoyed getting hot in the five different Jacuzzis. We had "fun, fun, fun," just like the Beach Boys' song—so much laughter. Breckenridge was at ten thousand feet in altitude, so we were huffing and puffing at times. But that was okay.

The day we went white water rafting was amazing. I didn't know what to expect. But it was fun. At times, I could see we would hit a big rock, but the water twirled us around and around like a big swirl. We did get stuck at one point against a big rock for a while, and we thought we were going to flop over. My thoughts went, *Wow, am I going to get thrown overboard, drenched in water?* That didn't happen, but the thrill of it all!

On another day, we went on ATVs. That was another exciting day. Fast and furious, we were driving over rocks, mud, and trenches, being thrown over bumps and bruises. We were going from an altitude of ten thousand feet to maybe thirteen thousand feet, seeing more snow and, at times, gushes of water.

On yet another day, we were all sitting on a deck next to a beautiful creek with crystal clear water, eating pizza. Then we walked along a beautiful street with beautiful flowers and beautiful shops. There was such beautiful scenery; the tops of the mountains had white snowcaps. The lakes had such crystal clear water with such beautiful reflections of the blue skies.

Again, the thought of heaven came into my mind. It was as if the Lord's Prayer came true: "Your Kingdom come, Your will be done on earth as it is Heaven." Yes, again, we were on earth, but it was like being in heaven. But this time, with kids and grandkids, we were all together. That was the beauty of it all. We were in such unity. So in heaven, we won't be alone. We will be in the great company of like-minded loved ones, no strangers, no enemies, just all loving one another, hugging each other, no fear of COVID-19 cases, no viruses to keep us six feet apart, no face masks, no protests, no protesters, just all loving one another. And with God, who is love, so much joy we will have.

One psalm that describes more powerfully is below, a song by King David:

> *How truly wonderful and delightful*
> *To see brothers and sisters living together in*
> *sweet unity!*
> *It's as precious as the sacred scented oil*
> *Flowing from the head of the high priest*
> *Aaron,*
> *Dripping down upon his beard and running*
> *all the way down*

To the hem of his priestly robes. (Psalm
133:1–3)

I wrote about a dream that I had a few months ago.
Just like that dream, this whole week in Breckenridge was
another dream. I was in the woods in the dream before,
and I was with another friend. We were under a huge tree
and proceeded to cross a large stream, but it was very shallow. The whole setting was beautiful. That dream came to
my mind. But now I can add more.

And I even thought, as I have said before, while enjoying hiking, it was heaven on earth. Now the thought was,
*Maybe there is more in heaven and heavenly white water raft-
ing! There could be horseback riding!* Yes, there are horses
mentioned in the last book of the Bible, in Revelations,
and they are said to be in heaven. So we could be riding
horses. Oh, what a thought!

Our vacations are usually short; the time together here
on earth is not that much. A week or two of vacations,
we do long for them, and we look forward to them. Then
we have all the great memories. *But when I go to heaven,
I always wonder, "If it is eternity, with so much time in my
hands, what would I be doing?"*

Now I know there will be forests in heaven. There will be white water rapids and meadows and meadows of green grass on which we can gallop on horses for miles and miles. Maybe there are heavenly ATVs. I let my imagination run wild. *Even if I drown, an angel will pick me up.* "*Have no fear,*" *the angel would say.*

It will be beautiful; I can go and do so many things I have dreamed of being able to do in heaven. When I'm galloping on a horse, there will be an angel to pick me up if I fall. I could go as fast as I could. I won't fear at all even if a bear or lion appears; it will be a friendly one. I can wrestle with them and play with them; they will all greet me instead of chase me. I will have all the time in heaven to enjoy nature. I can go camping for days, hike for days, go horseback riding for days, and go white water rafting for days… There will be no time limit' I'll have all the time I need.

Below is a passage in the Bible that relates to me so much.

> *As for us, we have all of these great witnesses who encircle us like clouds.*
> *So we must let go of every wound that has pierced us and the sin we so easily fall into.*

Then we will be able to run life's marathon race with passion and determination, for the path has been already marked out before us.

We look away from the natural realm, and we fasten our gaze onto Jesus, who birthed faith within us and who leads us forward into faith's perfection. (Hebrews 12:1–2 TPT)

One day, we will be that great cloud of witnesses. We need to run life's marathon now with passion and determination, for our path has been marked. Now we look away from the natural realm and fasten our gaze unto Jesus. But look at what is ahead. *Wonderful heaven is awaiting us. Breckenridge is just a glimpse. It is hardly a tiny glimpse compared to heaven. I will be so enthralled with what I will see.*

I had such a great time with all my family; it was a time beyond my imagination. *But to be with a great cloud of witnesses, what a day that will be. I'll get to see Moses, Elijah, David, Peter, and Paul, and I can keep on naming them one by one. But above all, Jesus, what a great time that will be.*

And that day, I will be with you along with that great cloud of witnesses, living in unity in heaven with all the loved ones and enjoying all the rewards and joys of life that only heaven could offer. How sweet it is!

I sing because I'm happy
I sing because I'm free
Heaven is a beautiful place
Where all of God's children are going to live up there
In a city so bright and fair
(Curtis B. Doss)

34

Joking with the King of Kings

It was a late afternoon in November of 2015. I walked from the family room to the kitchen to have a cup of tea. I seemed to have been deep in thought. I just sat on a bar stool in the kitchen. Suddenly I felt a nudge on my right shoulder. I was transported to the spirit realm, and I saw myself sitting next to Jesus. He nudged me, shoulder to shoulder. He was pushing me to the left. So I nudged Him back, pushing Him to my right. He was just like a close friend joking with me. I was suddenly laughing with Him. He was so happy that I could not resist laughing with Him. Jokingly, I was sitting so close to Jesus, again I nudged Him, shoulder to shoulder, pushing Him to the right. He was laughing at me. He didn't mind my nudging. He was telling jokes to me, and I was laughing. We were having such a good time, a great time. This lasted about five minutes, such a great time, I can never forget. Suddenly He was gone, and I was sitting by myself.

I didn't know Jesus was such a jovial guy, He was like a close friend, like a brother I had known for a long time.

I may have been in deep thought, but when He suddenly sat next to me and started nudging me, it took me totally by surprise.

But seeing Jesus so happy made me so happy.

Creator of the Universe sitting next to me, making jokes, so happy, didn't matter to Him my nudging Him, pushing Him, like a longtime close friend, rather He was enjoying it.

King of kings is always near me; I just didn't realize, He took me to His world, which is in the heavenly places as His Word says, "And God hath raised us up together, and made us sit together in heavenly places in Christ Jesus" (Ephesians 2:6 BRG).

Yes, I am seated together with Him, all the time, in the heavenly places. When I accept Him and become His child, God raised me and made me sit together with Jesus in the heavens, where there should be no worry and sorrow. He just showed up and made me so happy and joyful. I was deep in thought, but when He showed up, He changed my whole outlook.

He took me to His world, the heavenly places, which is joy and love.

My request to Him always, "Your will be it done on earth as it is Heaven" (Matthew 6:10p NKJV).

That is how I must be all the time; because He is always next to me, how soon do I forget. He showed up in person to remind me that He, with His joyful self, is always next to me.

Some worries in this life may be like a giant facing me, but He can do anything; nothing is hard for Him, especially like these days, COVID.

But that's going to pass. So why worry? So when I have a friend like that, do I need to worry? "Give all your worries to Him, because He cares for you" (1 Peter 5:7 ERV). Just give it to Him, as easy as that!

Can I not talk to Him who controls all things that bother me?

Can I not ask Him when facing situations? He who wants to joke with me also wants me to be happy. He knows who I am; He knows more about me than I do. He can listen to me and give me wisdom on what to do.

But then I need to trust Him. I may not hear Him physically, but by faith, I know He will guide me on what to do. I now remember the song I used to sing,

> I once was lost in sin, but Jesus took me in
> And then a little light from heaven filled
> my soul
> It bathed my heart in love and wrote my
> name above
> And just a little talk with Jesus made me
> whole.
> Now let us have a little talk with Jesus
> Let us tell him all about our troubles
> He will hear our faintest cry
> He will answer by and by
> Feel a little prayer wheel turning
> And you'll know a little fire is burning

You will find a little talk with Jesus makes
it right.
Sometimes the path seems dreary without
a ray of cheer
And then the clouds about me hide the
light of day
The mists in me rise and hide the stormy
skies
And just a little talk with Jesus clears the
way.
I may have doubts and fears, my eyes be
filled with tears
But Jesus is a friend who watches day and
night
I go to him in prayer, He knows my every
care
And just a little talk with Jesus makes it
right
Find a little talk with Jesus makes it right
And he makes everything right, right,
right.
(Cleavant Derricks)

So when something bothers me, instead of worrying, I can take it to Jesus, have a little talk with Jesus, tell Him about all my troubles, give it to Him to solve it for me, then trust and believe in Him to work it out for me. I don't stop there, but then I thank Him for it and get joyful again because He has my problem (not me); I look at His happy face.

He is smiling, so I also smile back at Him. "He will achieve infinitely more than your greatest request, your most unbelievable dream, and exceed your wildest imagination!" (Ephesians 3:20p PT). As long as I have my little talk with Jesus, He makes everything right, right, right.

What a privilege, what a divine appointment.

"Be cheerful with joyous celebration in every season of life. Let joy overflow, for you are united with the Anointed One!" (Philippians 4:4 Passion).

So I need to be joyful. He came to give me joy that overflows. That's what He showed me when He started nudging me. Instead of letting my thoughts wander away, I need to capture my thoughts, and I need to realize He is always next to me. I focus on Him, and He is a happy

Guy. The same passage, in a different translation, says the following:

> *Celebrate God all day, every day. I mean, revel in him! Make it as clear as you can, to all you meet that you're on their side, working with them and not against them. Help them see that the Master is about to arrive.*
>
> *He could show up any minute!*
>
> *Don't fret or worry. Instead of worrying, pray. Let petitions and praises shape your worries into prayers, letting God know your concerns. Before you know it, a sense of God's wholeness, everything coming together for good, will come and settle you down. It's wonderful what happens when Christ displaces worry at the center of your life.*
>
> (Philippians 4:4–7 The Message)

I looked at the dictionary, what *revel* means. It said, "Enjoy oneself in a lively and noisy way, make merry." I can be a worrier; I can get anxious. But suddenly, He just showed next to me, without me expecting Him. He just surprised me. Ever since then, I realized He is always next to me. He is a cheerful guy. He loves to joke with me. So we made a whole lot of merry. He loves to make me happy. He can displace my worry with joy, making it bright as soon as I realize as His presence is near.

The verse started, "Celebrate God all day"; why? Because I am His child. When my son was small, I love to throw him up in the air to hear him laugh. Was my son afraid as he goes up in the air, he may fall and hurt himself? No, He was laughing, just as I was laughing. We were making merry. So was Jesus to me. I am His child; He loves to make me laugh. He throws me up in the air. When I laugh, He loves to hear me laugh. Life may have ups and downs, but if it is Jesus that's holding me, I can laugh because the Creator of the Universe is holding me, and He laughs with me too.

Remember, last week, in my writing, I said all these blessings started after I started spending at least an hour reading the Bible and meditating on God's Word. He does speak to me every day in the mornings, which I enjoy. Then, there have also been pleasant surprises, like Jesus showing up suddenly. Life has pleasant surprises when I give Him more time. His Word says, "Your young men shall see visions, Your old men shall dream dreams" (Acts 2:17 NKJV).

So I can celebrate every day with Him because when I give Him all my worries, He gives me joy, laughter, and fun. What a bargain? So as I said last week, spending time in the Bible, when He talks to me, is so crucial to have a personal relationship with Him. I love what He did when He showed up as a surprise, and now I want to keep building on that intimacy with Him. My conversations and my relationship with Him get stronger. That's how I celebrate every day with joy, peace, love because He is so near and dear to me.

And then I look forward to the day, when I will be with Him in heaven. What a day that will be. Then I will see Him face to face all the time. This is what the Bible says, "I heard a loud shout from the throne, saying, 'Look, God's home is now among his people! He will live with them, and they will be his people. God himself will be with them'" (Revelations 21:3). I can't wait till that day to come. But in the meantime, I still know He is with me even though I can't see Him all the time. Still, I will joke with the King of kings, who is always with me!

<<Image: Emoji>>
"Rejoice in the Lord always: and again I
say, Rejoice" (Philippians 4:4 BRG).

35

The Bold Move: Sadness into Dancing!

There was a college student named John going to a university here. He always tried to study hard, but his memory wasn't always good in taking tests. He always took time to think hard about the questions in his exams. He was facing finals and had to take a two-hour test along with over two hundred other students. His professor was very rude and obnoxious. The exam started.

Every ten minutes from the start of the test, the professor would announce, with a booming voice, the time that was left until the end of the test. The test was a tough one, so most of the students sat through the whole two hours. So for the last five minutes, the professor started counting down, "Five minutes left!" Four...three...two...and finally, one minute left. Finally, he made a loud announcement that the test was over and for all to submit their papers to him upfront.

Everybody started lining up to give the papers to Professor Huber, but John kept on working on the answers. He had only finished two-thirds of his paper. Ten minutes went by, and John kept on finishing the answers; Huber was busy collecting the papers. There was still a big line of students handing over their papers. Twenty minutes went by, and John was still working on the answers. But Huber was busy stacking up all the papers. Thirty minutes went by before John was finally finished with all his answers and just as Professor Huber was ready to exit the exam hall, John approached the professor with his paper.

The professor yelled at John, "Don't you know that the test was over thirty minutes ago?"

John replied, "Do you know who I am?"

Huber was taken back, and his mind went blank.

He stared blankly at John, thinking who this could be and said, "No."

John asked him again, "Do you know my name?"

Huber's mind went blank again and said, "No."

The professor was so confused that he lost his train of thought. As he stared blankly, John quickly picked up half the stack of exam papers, quickly placed his paper in the middle of the stack, placed the upper stack over his paper, and quickly walked out.

Professor Huber was dumbfounded. Before he knew it, John had walked out and he didn't know where his paper was in the middle of the stack because he didn't know John's name. By the time the professor had realized what had happened, John was already gone.

Why did I tell this story? The moral of the story above isn't the extra time that John liberally took, but the bold move he undertook to avoid failure in his exam. I don't suggest that you do what John did. John was a rebel for his cause. But why the bold move?

I was bought up in India in the Anglican Church. Even as I was little, I joined the choir, and I was regular in going to church. I did read the Bible stories but more than that, I was not religious or got anything religious. But I enjoyed music and any music, church or otherwise, I would attend. I was in the choir most of the time, I remember. So one day in my high school years, I saw there was going to be a rally in downtown Madras, that had lot of music and it was free. So I told my parents, I was going there and went there.

I enjoyed that evening. Then I found out, there was one there every Saturday evening and it was always free. Interestingly, there were many from the UK and the USA and they were really good singers and musicians. It was little different kind of music that I was not used to, but I still enjoyed them. There was always a speaker who spoke every time after the music. So I listened each time. It was different from the church sermons and quite interesting. Very interesting speakers with different speeches every time.

The message was no matter who I was, I was not good enough to meet God's standards, and I cannot please God on my own. But God wanted to reach me, and that was why He sent Jesus, His Son to live among us about two thousand years ago, taught many parables, and healed all that wanted healing, but when He was about thirty-three years old, beat Him up, whipped Him with many stripes on His back and crucified Him. Jesus did all that for me, so when I accept Him and believed on Him, He took my blame on Him, He who was sinless took my sins on the cross. All I have to accept is that Jesus was crucified for me, confess my wrongs and sins to Him, and believe that He took my wrongs and sins on Himself.

"For God so loved the world that He gave His only begotten Son, that whoever believes in Him should not perish but have everlasting life" (John 3:16 NKJV).

Even as I had gone many Saturday evenings, that message was pounding on my heart. Many Saturday evening, there was an invitation to go forward to accept Jesus as my personal Savior. But I did not have the guts to go forward, even though I wanted to. What would people think, if I walked by myself, to go the front. I was not bold, but I chicken, if you wanted to call me. One Saturday, I was leaving the meeting, I was approached by a gentleman, who told me he had watched me come many Saturdays by myself. So He asked me whether I had accepted Jesus. I told him, I wanted to but never had the boldness to go forward, so even though I wanted to accept Jesus, I wasn't sure.

He said, that it is easy, he said he will pray to accept Christ and me to follow his prayer. I agreed, and I followed his prayer, word for word. And at the end, he said,

"Congratulations, Jey. You have accepted Christ, and now, you are a Child of God."

So even though, I was not as bold as the Calculus student, to walk down the aisle, but I did become a child of God, when someone else came along to help me out. Whether you are bold to make this decision to accept Jesus or not, this decision determines whether you can have eternal life and live in heaven or not. Please look at the next two verses after the one I had mentioned below.

> *For God did not send His Son into the world to condemn the world, but that the world through Him might be saved.*
> *He who believes in Him is not condemned; but he who does not believe is condemned already, because he has not believed in the name of the only begotten Son of God.*
> (John 3:17 and 18 NKJV)

It says, he who does not believe in Jesus is condemned already, because he has not believed in Jesus, the only begotten Son of God. I was very glad that I believed Him, all the chapters I have written, I am able to write because I accepted Jesus. I have enjoyed every moment, even in times of loneliness, sadness, happiness, dreams, things that yet to come, because Jesus has been with me since I accepted Him. Oh! What a difference!

That difference can happen in your life too! You can accept Jesus as your Savior too! Just pray, "Lord Jesus, You died for my sins and wrongdoings. I accept that You died for my sins. Please forgive me, and now I accept You as my Lord and Savior and have become Your child. Thanks so much. In Your name, I pray. Amen!"

Now you believe that God has forgiven you for all the wrongs you have done, and you can become a child of God. If you have taken that step, please try to share with at least one person this important step you have taken. Please let me know of your decision to make this decision on my website at the back of the book, and I will send you a Bible and tools to help you study the Bible.

There was another step that happened and that was the infilling of the Holy Spirit. Jesus had said to His disciples that He left, He would leave the Holy Spirit as a Comforter and Helper in their lives. To me, that didn't happen in a dramatic way but in a very subtle way. As I read John 11, 12, and 14, I realized how important it was to have Him in my life. Every time, I needed wisdom in the things I had to do, He was there with me, subtly guiding me, giving me comfort and direction in all that I did. Especially as I read God's Word, he gave me new revelations, and it was sometimes, someone talking to me and I knew that I knew, it was the Holy Spirit. Even many of the chapter I had written was by His guidance, He showed me the Biblical verses to use. What a friend He has been to me.

Another bold step that I made that made a lot of difference in my life was my decision to read the Bible, God's Word for at least an hour each day. I couldn't be more happy than I have ever been since I made that decision. Oh! How I love the Bible. Every day, the Holy Spirit talks to me and I get fresh revelation every day, so I am in His Hands all the time. I have shared the dreams I have had, the visions of His presence next to me, and so much more. A lot of them are my personal stories only He and I can share with each other. I can agree with David so well as He writes, in Psalms 16:5 to 11 (ERV):

> *Lord, you give me all that I need.*
> *You support me.*
> *You give me my share.*
> *My share is wonderful.*

My inheritance is very beautiful.
I praise the Lord because He taught me well.
Even at night He put his instructions deep
inside my mind.
I always remember that the Lord is with me.
He is here, close by my side,
so nothing can defeat me.
So my heart and soul will be very happy.
Even my body will live in safety,
because you will not leave me in the place of
death.
You will not let your faithful one rot in the
grave.
You will teach me the right way to live.
Just being with you will bring complete
happiness.
Being at your right side will make me happy
forever."

Yes, being with the Lord will bring me complete happiness, being next to Him makes me happy forever.

What else do I want. This is heaven on earth. This way, the Lord has seated me together with Jesus in the heavenly places.

"Yes, it is because we are a part of Christ Jesus that God raised us from death and seated us together with Him in the Heavenly Places" (Ephesians 2:6 ERV).

Yes, we are seated together with Jesus in heavenly places all the time, where I am, in whatever circumstances I am in, in whatever I face, I am in heaven, even though physically, I am on earth, and that is my mindset, I am no more in sorrow, I am always rejoicing and I am always dancing in my spirit where my Holy Spirit are joined together as one.

> *You have changed my sorrow into dancing.*
> *You have taken away my sackcloth*
> *and clothed me with joy.*
> *You wanted me to praise You and not be*
> *silent.*
> *Lord my God, I will praise You forever!*
> (Psalms 30:11–12 ERV)

I feel the sweetness of His love
Piercing my darkness,
I see the bright and morning sun
As it ushers in His joyful gladness!
Chorus:

He's turned my mourning into dancing again

He's lifted my sorrows, I can't stay silent

I must sing for His joy has come.

(Walker Tommy)

36

Be Alert and Prepared

This story below was already in a previous chapter, but this has a different ending. Usually, on New Year's Eve, we used to plan to have a party. We used to have international students in our home every week. The students came from various countries and every year. The students changed. Sometimes half of the group stayed, but it varied. We would always provide dinner whether it was thirty or sixty people. It is hard to mention all that happened, but I will try to talk about some interesting and funny things happened along the way.

On one New Year's Eve, it was a fun night playing games till midnight. We all planned to stay awake till midnight, greet each other for the New Year, then all go to sleep. Everyone slept mainly in the living room either on sleeping bags or the carpeted floors, got up at about

5:30 a.m., got dressed up, and headed for the Rose Parade in Pasadena. Everything was going as planned, and there were about fifty to sixty students that New Year's Eve, as I remembered. And one of the leaders, Ben, an ardent hiker, stood and asked whether the students would be interested in a night hike after midnight. Many students thought it was very adventurous and said they would be interested.

About twenty students raised their hands. So I told them, if they were going, they should all come back before 5:30 a.m. so we could all go as a group to Rose Parade. They all agreed. So the midnight hour came, and we all greeted each other. And the group of twenty students left for the night hike. The rest of us got into bed, turned off the lights, and went to sleep. We left the front door open so the twenty night hikers could get back in the house.

My daughter had gone for the New Year's Eve party and came back after we had all gone to sleep. She didn't know anything about twenty night hikers and locked the front door behind her. All the twenty night hikers came back at about 4:00 a.m., cold and shivering, wanting to get back to the house's heat. But when they tried to open the door, thinking it would be open, they found it locked. Then they frantically rang the doorbell. But everyone inside was so sound asleep that nobody got up to open the door for them. So the gang of twenty had to stand up in the cold outside, still shivering. The alarm inside rang at 5:30 a.m., and someone inside switched on the living room light.

The gang of twenty saw the light inside and madly rang the doorbell, and finally, the door opened. Then it was time to get dressed, get into the cars, and head to the Rose Parade. The twenty did not get any sleep at all and started to sleep in the cars on the way to the Rose Parade. But that was only, like, forty minutes. Then there was a long walk to find a place to sit and watch the parade. It was still cold. But we had to carry all the chairs and other goodies like food, blankets, etc. to where we were seated. Finally, we found a place to sit at about 7:30 am. And the parade started at about 8:30 am.

But the twenty, after they got the seats, all went to sleep because they never got any sleep all night and were all so tired. So the parade came, and we all, including the thirty, enjoyed the parade, but the twenty were sound asleep during the whole parade. We never could ask the twenty night hikers how the night hike was because they were sound asleep. These are some of the fun things that happened during the years of our international-student meetings in our house.

This reminds me of a story that Jesus said to His disciples:

> *When my coming draws near, heaven's kingdom realm can be compared to ten maidens who took their oil lamps and went outside to meet the bridegroom and his bride. Five of them were foolish and ill-prepared, for they took no extra oil in their lamps. Five of them were wise, for they took flasks of olive oil with their lamps. When the bridegroom didn't come when they expected, they all grew drowsy and fell asleep.*
>
> *Then suddenly, in the middle of the night, they were awakened by the shout "Get up! The bridegroom is here! Come out and have an encounter with him!" So all the girls got up and trimmed their lamps. But the foolish ones were running out of oil, so they said to the five wise ones, "Share your oil with us, because our lamps are going out!"*

"We can't," they replied. "We don't have enough for all of us. You'll have to go and buy some for yourselves!"

While the five girls were out buying oil, the bridegroom appeared. Those who were ready and waiting were escorted inside with him and the wedding party to enjoy the feast. And then the door was locked. Later, the five foolish girls came running up to the door and pleaded, "Lord, Lord, let us come in!"

But he called back, "Go away! Do I know you? I can assure you, I don't even know you!"

"That is the reason you should always stay awake and be alert because you don't know the day or the hour when the Bridegroom will appear." (Matthew 25:1–13 TPT)

That was Jesus telling a parable to His disciples. When Ben took his group at night, I didn't think they were prepared if the door would be closed when they got back. So they were caught being in the cold outside, freezing when they got back. So they never got to enjoy the beautiful Rose Parade.

As Jesus was telling His disciples about Himself being the Bridegroom, He said He would be back again. See the two verses below. He is the Son of Man coming back to take back with Him the wise and those prepared to meet Him as a child of God. He warned everyone whether they would stay awake and be alert. Would you be wise, or are you a foolish one if He comes back in 2022?

> *Jesus answered him, "You just said it yourself. And more than that, you are about to see the Son of Man seated at the right hand of God, the Almighty. And one day, you will also see the Son of Man coming in the heavenly clouds!"* (Matthew 26:64 TPT)

> *Jesus answered him, "I am. And more than that, you are about to see the Son of Man seated at the right hand of the Almighty and coming in the heavenly clouds!"* (Mark 14:62 TPT)

This book has a lot of Bible quotations. For those who do not have a Bible, but want one, the Author is willing to send a Bible. For those who want to receive a Bible, please send an email with an address to SorrowIntoDancing@gmail.com.

For those who may have questions or comments, please send them to SorrowIntoDancing@gmail.com.

About the Author

The author grew up in India and eventually settled in California. You will find out from reading the book how that all happened. This is his biography. He did his bachelor of architecture in University of Madras, India, and his masters of architecture at Pratt in New York. Most of his biography is in the book, and you will find out quite a bit about him, reading it.

He has California licenses as an architect, as a contractor, and in real estate. He did his first book about ten years ago entitled *Feel Awesome*, and this is his second one. He is married and has two daughters and one son.

CPSIA information can be obtained
at www.ICGtesting.com
Printed in the USA
BVHW041154071222
653658BV00001B/1